The Greatest

Manifestation
Principle
in the World

*The Missing Secret Behind
the Law of Attraction That
Will Enable You to Finally
Manifest Your Desires*

Carnelian Sage

Think-Outside-the-Book
PUBLISHING, INC.

Publisher:

Think-Outside-the-Book
PUBLISHING, INC.

311 N. Robertson Boulevard, Suite 323
Beverly Hills, California 90211
http://www.GreatestManifestationPrinciple.com

Dedication

To ZD
for loving without fear
for loving without expectation of reciprocity
for letting me know love's pathway to God
and for teaching me that to love is to live.

And to God
whose truth is the essence of all creation
and manifestation.

 Chapter 1

Is the Law of Attraction a Hoax or a Real Treasure?

*I*magine how your life would be if you could manifest all your desires into existence. What if all you had to do was wish for a loving relationship, an ideal job, perfect health, your dream house, a luxurious vacation, a brand new car—or anything you want—and it magically materialized in your life?

This is the promise of the Law of Attraction. That is why millions of people have been *seduced* by its lure—and have devoured books, DVDs and courses that promise to show them how to use this "scientific law" that can bring wealth, health and all the good things in life.

Perhaps the question you need to ask is this: Have you—or anyone you know—actually seen the amazing results that you're *supposed* to be getting in your life by practicing the principles of the Law of Attraction **as it**

is currently taught? Have you acquired the new car and the beautiful house, achieved abundant wealth or been healed of an incurable disease—or are you one of the majority who has learned to *patiently* wait for your desires to manifest?

If so, be prepared for a *long wait*.

The fact is, your chances of getting what you want by using the prevailing teachings of the Law of Attraction are about as slim as winning a million dollars in a Las Vegas casino. It's a gamble—and the odds are stacked against you. (I'll give you evidence of this in a moment.)

If, on the other hand, you'd like to discover the **missing secret** and the *real power* behind the Law of Attraction that will enable you to truly manifest all your heart's desires, you'll find the answer in this book. In the latter part of this chapter, I'll show you...

... the long and convoluted journey I took before I finally discovered this missing secret

... why practicing the Law of Attraction has always been an exercise in trial-and-error and hits-or-misses for most people—with more errors and misses than successes

... how I learned the greatest manifestation principle that successful people have used *in conjunction with the Law of Attraction* (the principle that they didn't even realize was the real reason for their success); and

... why no one is talking about this principle until now.

When you discover this powerful principle, you will ...

- find the "wormhole" between the emotional and the spiritual dimensions—the interface that turns desires from their unformed potentiality to actualization

- understand how simply changing your attitude about your desire dramatically increases the likelihood of manifesting your desire

- notice that the right people, the right resources, the right breaks and the right circumstances just magically appear in your life without any prompting or effort from you

- spontaneously behave in ways that enable you to naturally lose excess weight, eliminate procrastination, get rid of mental obsessions or addictions, resolve marital and personal relationship problems—and rise above any and all human dilemmas

- learn how to make others feel energized, feel better about themselves, be more loving and at peace with the world just by being in your vicinity

- learn how to heal yourself of an ailment, disease or illness by amplifying the power of the manifestation principle to a level wherein sickness disappears; and

- enter the realm where miracles become an everyday occurrence.

To provide you with a foretaste of the information you're about to discover, I present you with the following:

There is an infinite field of energy that surrounds and permeates all things, embodying all existence, both seen and unseen. Some call this energy field Source Energy, the quantum field, divine intelligence, the universal mind, the field of all possibilities—or its ultimate name, God. This field is without beginning or end, goes beyond time and space, and consists of pure boundless, immeasurable power and energy, vibrating higher and faster than the ordinary levels of human intellect and awareness can observe, comprehend or explain.

In this formless vibratory spiritual field of Infinite Potentiality lie all the hopes and dreams of all mankind—where all your desires are already an unformed potentiality waiting to manifest into existence. All human beings exist within this field, are part of it, and are connected to it—but most of us have lost our natural connection to it because of the emergence of the ego. The ego is your false self, an illusory idea that you construct in your consciousness about who and what you are. It is your ego that keeps you separate from this field, and makes you unable to access the field's power to bring you what you desire.

You can take anything you desire from formless to concrete expression simply by reconnecting with this field. The attainment of your desires, then, comes from not allowing your ego to think that it can cause things to happen or attract things to you by simply focusing on positive thoughts and feelings. It is when you transcend your ego, let go of your desires, and stay in harmony with this field, that your desires can and MUST necessarily manifest into existence.

The greatest manifestation principle in the world that is revealed in this book will enable you to realign yourself and stay in harmony with this field where all things are possible.

I invite you to read this book repeatedly and often. Simply reading a chapter, a page or even a paragraph from this book everyday will have a *transformational effect*—it will make you a different person and will have a profound impact on your energy level and personal growth. As you read and reflect on the material contained herein, layers of wisdom and insights will unfold that will accelerate your ability to effortlessly attract the things you *really* want. When you allow the power of the greatest manifestation principle in the world to permeate your awareness, amazing things will begin to manifest in every area of your life.

It is my hope that this book spares you the dis-illusionment and disappointment you might experience as you practice the Law of Attraction **the way it is currently being taught**. May the spiritual truth and the expansive way of seeing things that you will discover in this book enable you not only to manifest your desires but allow you to find unbounded joy, love and peace in your life's journey.

Chapter 2

How to Go from Wanting to Having

*T*he popularity of the Law of Attraction has reached fever pitch ever since the 2006 release of the video titled, *The Secret* (and the book of the same title), as well as the publication of recent bestselling book titles such as *Ask and It is Given, Excuse Me Your Life is Waiting, The Amazing Power of Deliberate Intent,* and *The Law of Attraction.*

In writing this book, it is not my intention to make moral or ethical judgments about the spirit in which the current body of knowledge relating to the Law of Attraction was compiled and presented. The concepts currently presented, such as *visualization of desire* and *gratitude for what one has* are useful and important. If all that the **current teaching** of the Law of Attraction accomplishes is to get people to focus on positive things, and things that make them feel good; allow them to focus on the things they want (instead of focus on what they don't want); eliminate their "why do bad things always happen to me" victim attitude; and inspire and empower them to take charge of their thoughts and their destiny, it has provided a beneficial service.

But if the Law of Attraction concepts lead people to believe that the universe is like a cosmic restaurant that takes your orders and delivers them to you just as surely as a waiter delivers the food you ordered to your table, that's surely an exercise in delusion. The current books, courses and DVDs have made people as delusional as the fairy tale emperor who paraded around town thinking he was dressed in the most elegant attire the world has ever seen, when in actuality he had no clothes on! (See Hans Christian Andersen's *The Emperor's New Clothes*)

My motivation for writing this book is predicated on my devotion to the pursuit and dissemination of truth. Since a record number of people are flocking to the Law of Attraction now more than ever before in history, I didn't want to see all these people spend years like I did, trying to manifest their desires but becoming disillusioned when nothing happened.

The objective of this book is to correct any

inaccuracies, point out hidden dangers, dispel myths surrounding the Law of Attraction—and more importantly, shed light on the most powerful manifestation principle in the world that no one is talking about. When you use this powerful manifestation principle in your practice of the Law of Attraction, you enter the realm of miracles where the manifestation of all desires is truly possible.

This book is purposely brief because the greatest manifestation principle in the world is quite simple, as all great truths are. Although I refer to it as the "missing secret," it has actually never been a secret at all. It is a *spiritual truth* that has been used by ancient mystics to modern-day spiritual seekers to people of all faiths—and everyone in between—with great success. But no one has ever discovered how to use that spiritual truth *in conjunction with* the Law of Attraction to make the manifestation of desires a *certainty*, instead of something merely *hoped for*—until now.

The case histories I have studied of people that managed to succeed in manifesting their desires through the Law of Attraction invariably had this manifestation principle in place—but weren't aware that it was this manifestation principle that materialized their desires. A well-known motivational speaker, who has achieved great success and abundant wealth, unconsciously uses this principle. Although his teachings encompass various techniques involving quantum physics, spiritual truths and the Law of Attraction, it was this one principle in particular that allowed all good things to continually show up in his life.

This is the reason why some people are astonishingly successful in manifesting desires—but most are not successful at all. Somewhere along the way, those who are successful somehow hook up with the greatest manifestation principle *without knowing it*—and that principle supplies the missing ingredient that completes the recipe for manifestation.

And *voila*! Their desires are manifested—and they're justifiably elated. However, since they are unaware of the real reason why their desire manifested, they erroneously assume it was because they focused on what they wanted; took their focus away from the things they didn't want; visualized their desire until it was so real they could almost touch it; and expressed gratitude every step of the way. Sadly, although this popular ask-believe-receive "formula" for manifesting desires seems to make sense—and is even supposedly supported by "hard science" and Scripture—it is <u>not</u> what causes desires to manifest.

That's why oftentimes, when people who were successful at manifesting one desire try to duplicate their success using the "formula" they implemented before, they fail to produce the same successful results —and their desire does not manifest the second time around and beyond. That's also why in over 100 years that the Law of Attraction has been in the public eye, there has never been any degree of consistency or certainty when it comes to getting results with its use.

The practice of the Law of Attraction, if based on the teachings of the books, courses and DVDs released in the last 100 years, has about as much chance of manifesting one's desires as a person who dreams of becoming a movie star has in making his or her dream come true. The Law of Attraction employs a *hit-or-miss methodology* that has been passed down through the years. Some practitioners report positive results (most of which have nothing to do with the attraction principle—see Chapter 2) but the majority experience little or no results. Most of the failures are never reported, which explains why most people are unaware of the dismal success rate (or conversely, the alarming failure rate) of those who practice the Law of Attraction.

Therein lies the partial truth in practically every concept known to man. People take their limited understanding of something and represent it to others as *the* truth. The people who are exposed to the distorted information, in turn, represent it to others as *the* truth. Ultimately, all we really have is fractured versions of the truth—all of us knowing a small part but never the whole. And you know what they say about people knowing just enough to be dangerous!

The Law of Attraction is not unlike the elephant encountered by the six blind men in the famous Indian legend. The story talks about six blind men giving their own individual assessments of an elephant. The first one happened to fall against the broad and sturdy side of the elephant, and concluded that the elephant is very much like a wall. The second one, feeling the tusk, said the elephant was very much like a spear. The third one happened to take the squirming trunk in his hands, and said the elephant was very much like a snake. The fourth one, reached out and touched the elephant's knee, and concluded that the elephant is very much like a tree. The fifth one happened to touch the ear, and insisted that the elephant is very much like a fan. And the sixth one seized the swinging tail, and said the elephant is very much like a rope. Each one of them was partly right—but at the same time, mostly wrong. The comical part of it all is that their dispute stemmed from utter ignorance because none had ever *seen* an elephant!

Over the last 100 years, people have formed their opinions about this thing called the Law of Attraction, formulating their own compartmentalized theories as to what makes it work—and never hitting on the truth. This book then is the first to remove the blindfold from the world's current understanding of the Law of Attraction and reveal the true power behind it so that people can finally experience spectacular and consistent results from it.

My Journey to the Ethereal

The concept of manifesting desires has been a great interest of mine since 1981. I've studied the principles of quantum physics and its much heralded offshoot, the

Law of Attraction, for years. I was searching for that secret alchemy that would turn thoughts into things. Its promise was too irresistible and intriguing to ignore. It seemed like the next best thing to having a magic wand that you can wave and cause your wishes to come true.

The Law of Attraction *appeared* to have the answer to my quest. Little did I know that there was a mysterious power behind it that I wasn't destined to discover until 21 years later. This mysterious power was one that no one had ever included in any discussion of the Law of Attraction I'd ever encountered—and one without which the Law of Attraction seldom works.

It is to the illumination of this real secret behind the Law of Attraction that this book is lovingly dedicated. For over 20 years, I researched and investigated all known avenues of manifestation including quantum mechanics, paranormal studies, esoteric sciences, affirmation techniques, hypnosis, Scriptural secrets and everything else in between. By the start of this new millennium, I had acquired enough information about manifestation and the Law of Attraction to become a lay expert on the subject. And yet all that knowledge has gotten me no closer to manifesting my desires into existence. Apart from small victories like finding ideal parking spaces and experiencing a sprinkling of minor pleasant occurrences (that might have been the result of confirmation bias or the *experimenter effect* discussed in the next chapter), I had yet to find evidence that one could truly alchemize one's thoughts into reality.

It was rather peculiar that back in 1997 when I aggressively practiced everything I knew about the Law of Attraction, I suffered the most severe financial setback in my life and I came close to bankruptcy. I would have declared bankruptcy had it not been for the financial help of a loved one who bailed me out temporarily. That ensuing financial slump and career meltdown lasted for four years even as I continued to apply the principles of the Law of Attraction and immerse myself in positive thoughts. I couldn't understand why this was happening and why I wasn't attracting the prosperity I desired.

Several years ago, I underwent an ultrasound scan, and several tumors were found in my body. Once again, I used the principles of the Law of Attraction combined with healthy eating habits to make them disappear and avert the need for the major surgery that my doctor urged me to have. I had also read about the healing power of laughter in the late Dr. Norman Cousins's book, so I watched funny TV shows and movies whenever I could—all to no avail. I immersed myself in positive thoughts and practiced a healthy lifestyle, but one of the tumors grew to the size of a small grapefruit within a matter of weeks!

I couldn't believe it was happening to me!

As a result of the tumors, I became so weak that I was rushed to the Emergency Room at a nearby hospital on two occasions, and had to endure two separate inpatient stays within two weeks of each other. I finally had to agree to undergo major surgery to remove the tumors, all of which were benign, thank God.

That setback was probably the pivotal point in my adventures (and misadventures) with the Law of Attraction. I began to ponder the reasons why I was not getting the results I desired. For that matter, I took a long, hard look at the reasons why all the people I've known, who were using the principles of the Law of Attraction (including many individuals who *teach* the principles), were still struggling financially and weren't getting as much out of life as they pretended they were getting.

I began to wonder whether the Law of Attraction was just a hoax after all.

A Law-of-Attraction-aficionado colleague of mine not only did not achieve the successful business enterprise that he visualized everyday, but instead found himself in a long string of disastrous events that led to a debt of over $200,000.

A friend of mine, who's a perennially high-energy individual, has used the Law of Attraction for a year to get a better job so that she won't have to wait on tables at a restaurant—and she's still stuck in that job today. To make matters worse, the restaurant cut back her hours, which left her struggling financially to make ends meet. Try as she might, she can't seem to find another job. Her other desire is to break into the acting field. She's been visualizing herself as a successful working actress, but none of her positive thoughts have landed her a single role, even after endless auditions.

A female singer-songwriter acquaintance has always dreamed of winning a Grammy award for her music.

She's been visualizing herself accepting a Grammy Award—and her vision is so vivid that she even has her acceptance speech all planned out. She's been using the Law of Attraction since 2004, and she has yet to see any evidence that her dream will ever happen.

A man that I met recently said he had watched the film documentary, *The Secret*, a year ago and has been enthusiastically practicing the principles for several months. His desire has always been to get out of his dead-end job and start his own lucrative business enterprise. He's still waiting.

A married couple has been using the Law of Attraction to have their application for a home loan approved, but after months of visualizing and engaging in positive thoughts, their application for a modest home loan was denied.

I can give hundreds of examples of failed attempts to manifest desires by people who have used the Law of Attraction for a few months to several years.

In over two decades of investigating manifestation principles, I've met countless people who, like me, had started out practicing the Law of Attraction enthusiastically—only to be disappointed by the lack of results. I can tell you quite honestly that for every individual that has reportedly succeeded in manifesting what they desired by using the current *hit-or-miss methodology* of the Law of Attraction, I can show you at least 1,000 who have not manifested their desires into their lives.

In the field of clinical investigation, when only one out of 1,000 test subjects responds favorably to a test substance, this 0.1% success rate is considered clinically insignificant enough not to warrant further investigation. Oftentimes the single test subject that did respond favorably did so because of some extraneous variables, a fluke, or the placebo effect. In *The Science of Getting Rich*, a book written by Wallace Wattles and published back in 1910 (and which inspired the making of *The Secret*), the author claimed that when one practices the attraction principle, "Failure is impossible." I don't know about you, but the 0.1% success rate I've observed is a far cry from the 100% success rate Wattles suggests. Sadly, the probability of failure is astronomically high. Failure comes 99.9% of the time unless you apply the greatest manifestation principle in the world.

Let's get real. If failure is indeed an impossibility, and the Law of Attraction principles have been around since the early 20th century for people to practice, wouldn't we have a legion of wealthy people in this world instead of just a small handful? Shouldn't the majority of the people who practice the Law of Attraction already have manifested their desires—and shouldn't we now have a planet full of happy people with joyful relationships with each other?

It might be pointed out that it's not for lack of trying since millions of people have faithfully followed these principles for decades and are still left wondering why they are not yet rich, are still in poor health, still don't have the dream house, dream car, dream job or dream relationship they've been focusing on for a long time.

Some would have you believe that the reason why that isn't so is because the Law of Attraction has been shrouded in secrecy for many centuries, and has been suppressed by those who don't want others to have the secret power. I'm afraid this simply isn't true.

The Law of Attraction has never been kept a secret from anybody. One of the earliest known references to the Law of Attraction dates back to a book published in 1906 titled *Thought Vibration or the Law of Attraction in the Thought World* by William Walker Atkinson. That book, or the information in it, was never suppressed nor spoken about only in hushed circles. Neither has Wallace Wattles's 1910 classic, *The Science of Getting Rich* been kept secret. Both books were freely distributed and the drama of secrecy has been overly exaggerated.

The secrecy or non-secrecy is immaterial, however, if we can't prove that the Law of Attraction is effective in manifesting desires at all.

In my experience, the Law of Attraction does work —but not when it's practiced in the manner described in the entire body of knowledge available today. In fact, not a single book, course, CD or DVD ever produced in this or any other century contains the missing manifestation principle behind the Law of Attraction. I found that missing principle by accident.

I recently attended a lecture given by someone whom I consider to be one of the most deeply spiritual individuals I have ever encountered. The lecture was not about manifestation but rather about spiritual truths that can be applied to our everyday lives. One of the truths he revealed struck a chord in me. It was so profound in its simplicity, and yet wielded more power than anything I could imagine. I began to wonder whether it was the secret to manifesting one's desires.

I examined the spiritual truth in light of the recent events of my life. In 2002, I had just begun to recover from the 4-year financial slump I had referred to earlier, and for some reason, I had begun to experience unexpected success in every area of my life. My income multiplied by a factor of 5 in a matter of months. I rekindled a broken relationship with my ex-spouse, and our relationship has become the blissful and enduring one I've always wanted. People and resources that I needed for the accomplishment of my goals, appeared miraculously in my life at the right time, as if on cue. I was able to afford to live in a pricey high-rise residence with a magnificent view. I was also able to buy a brand new luxury car (whereas I had only been able to afford previously owned automobiles before). My credit score suddenly leaped from the low 500s to the high 700s. I established a business enterprise that brought in a substantial, effortless income that affords me the luxury of not having to work another day, if I don't want to. I authored 5 books in 4 years. But the best thing of all was that I experienced a deep joy that surpassed anything I could have received from the material rewards that the universe was giving me.

I looked at all I had accomplished from 2002 to 2006 —and I discovered something truly wonderful. In every one of the instances wherein my desire manifested into reality, that spiritual truth—the secret ingredient, if you will—was present.

In examining the successes of people who have managed to get significant results from practicing the Law of Attraction, I observed that this spiritual truth was also an essential factor in the manifestation of their desires. Usually, they didn't even realize that they were exercising the power of that spiritual truth, and weren't even aware it had anything to do with the materialization of their desire.

Individuals of great accomplishment throughout human history have also invariably aligned themselves with this spiritual truth. Whenever they attributed the source of their power to *something greater than themselves*, more often than not, it was this manifestation principle that was at the heart of their success. The same is true of individuals who have been miraculously healed of lingering—and even terminal— illnesses.

A mother of three boys, whom I will call Abigail, was struggling to make ends meet. Her husband had lost his job, and she had been thrust into the role of bread-winner overnight. One day, as Abigail was uncon-sciously practicing the manifestation principle which I referred to earlier, she got a call from Bill, the father of one of her son's friends, who offered her a sales job with his company. Abigail was a secretary by profession, earning $2,500 a month. She had never had a sales job in her life, but she decided to bite the bullet and accept the commission-only job because she knew if she stayed in her secretarial job, there was no way she would be able to pay the bills, feed her family and keep their modest 3-bedroom house in the suburbs of Chicago. In the meantime, she continued practicing the manifestation principle every single day, not realizing it would contribute to her success. A few months after she became a sales rep, she became the highest sales producer, earning more than $25,000 in commissions every month, thereby multiplying her former income by 10. Her husband found a high-paying job after being unemployed 6 months, and soon thereafter, they were able to buy a 5-bedroom $1.2 million house in a prestigious gated community.

A woman from California, whom I will call Sylvia, was diagnosed with Stage 4 cancer (lymphoma). At the advice of her oncologist, Sylvia started undergoing chemotherapy. After suffering severe adverse effects from only 2 sessions, she stopped chemo altogether, and her doctor was concerned about the prognosis of her cancer. Sylvia began *unconsciously* practicing the manifestation principle, unaware that it would have any impact on her illness. During her subsequent screening, no trace of cancer was found in her. Her oncologist was amazed over her spontaneous recovery from cancer.

A woman named Susan was having a rocky relationship with her boyfriend, Mark. After dating for 2 years, Susan and Mark got engaged to be married, but Mark broke off the engagement after 3 months. Susan was never really convinced that Mark loved her, and whenever she asked him if he did, he would always give an ambiguous answer like "I do love you at a certain level." That was no comfort to her, but she kept praying and practicing the Law of Attraction in hopes that he would want to commit to her one day. Then, without deliberate purpose, she began *unconsciously* practicing the manifestation principle (unaware of its power), and a few months later, a miraculous change came over Mark. He began expressing an undying love for her, told her he never loved a woman the way he loved her. One day, she was startled when she overheard him telling his friend that she was the only woman he would be willing to die for.

When I discovered the effect of this manifestation principle, I was overwhelmed by the staggering and miraculous implications that it would have on people's lives and the world. Tears of joy came pouring out of my eyes out of gratitude for the gift of spiritual discernment and the realization of this truth.

I call this spiritual truth the greatest manifestation principle in the world. It has removed all doubt in my mind that the Law of Attraction, *when combined with this manifestation principle*, does work. I can tell you with complete truthfulness that it does work—but only when this missing secret is applied. The mechanism by which it works goes well beyond the scope and measurement of science and mathematics and lies in the nonlinear, ethereal realm. Therefore, I urge you to view it not from the standpoint of traditional or quantum physics, but invite you instead to test the principle and prove to yourself that it certainly works in ways that go far beyond your expectations.

Chapter 3

The Myths and Dangers Behind the Law of Attraction

*P*rior to the release of the video, *The Secret*, in 2006, great interest had already been previously generated about manifesting one's desires through the use of the Law of Attraction. Bestselling books and courses have brought about renewed attention to the Law of Attraction in recent years.

The self-help industry has been publishing books about this principle for decades, but the books have not necessarily referred to it as the "Law of Attraction." It has been called a gamut of things including "positive thinking," the "attraction principle," "thought vibration," "the power of emotions," or a close cousin, the "power of affirmations."

Before revealing the spiritual truth behind the greatest manifestation principle in the world, it is necessary to give a brief summary of the mechanics of the Law of Attraction the way it is currently taught. We can then deconstruct it, eliminate its weak, ineffective and untrue elements, and use it as a basis for discussing the manifestation method that works.

What is the Law of Attraction — and How Does It Work?

The Law of Attraction is governed by the principle that *like attracts like*. Simply stated, you attract to your life anything you give your energy, focus and attention to—whether wanted or unwanted. What you think about is what you create; what you give out is what you get back.

Everything in the universe, including our thoughts —are made of energy which reverberates at specific vibrational frequencies. Different kinds of thoughts generate different kinds of vibrations, and vibrations of thought can actually be photographed (*From Enigma to Science*, by George W. Meek, Samuel Weiser Inc. 1977). Positive thoughts have a high vibrational frequency, which means the waves move at a higher and faster rate.

According to those who teach the Law of Attraction, positive thoughts attract everything in the universe that is a vibrational match to your thoughts—and that means everything from the best parking spaces to a diamond necklace to a dream car or house. Negative thoughts, on the other hand, have a low vibrational frequency, which means the waves move at a lower and slower rate. Therefore, they attract everything in the universe that's a vibrational match to those thoughts— and that means everything from a stopped up sink to getting into a car accident, getting fired from a job, getting sick, and so on.

The proponents of the Law of Attraction insist that the reason people get unfortunate or unpleasant circumstances in life—illness or poor health, poverty, disaster, etc.—is because they attracted such things through their negative thoughts. They claim that the way to change that is by not focusing on the things one does *not* want, but focusing on the things one *does* want instead.

Some teachers of the Law of Attraction even go to the extent of saying that if you spend anywhere from 15 to 17 seconds of pure, focused attention on what you want, uninterrupted by negative thoughts and emotions, that's the equivalent of an entire day's worth of activity towards the accomplishment of the things you want.

So ... does the practice of the Law of Attraction really manifest one's desires as described above?

First, let us identify the dangers and myths surrounding the Law of Attraction so that we can unearth the parts of it that we can use for our benefit.

The Hidden Dangers of Practicing the Law of Attraction

The critics of the Law of Attraction regard it as a repackaged version of the age-old positive thinking principles. While there's nothing wrong with positive thinking—and it is, in fact, a widely accepted mainstay in the field of self-improvement and alternative health—its proponents often propagate myths, half truths, and sometimes, even falsehoods that could potentially damage people's lives. Those myths, half truths and falsehoods largely go unchecked because the Law of Attraction is neither provable nor refutable in the intellectual sense.

Some myths start quite innocently. For example, someone states a premise or a theory in a book published a century ago. Then, someone from this century takes the premise out of context; presents it to a new audience as a fact (instead of a theory); the audience accepts the fact without verifying its accuracy; and before long, an entire body of information emerges that presents as fact that which was only a theory, or possibly a falsehood. Sometimes books are written, entire countries are governed, and people's lives are changed (for better or for worse) because of myths that were inappropriately reported as truth. It's not unlike the telephone game, wherein each participant secretly whispers to the next a phrase or sentence whispered to them by the preceding participant, thereby creating cumulative errors in the process. When you rise above the comical aspect of the game and realize the dangerous inaccuracies of rumors, we see that it's no laughing matter.

Therefore, before you buy into the popular premise that is the Law of Attraction, let's separate fact from fiction.

Myth No. 1: **The Law of Attraction is a universal law that is backed by hard science. It is an elemental law of physics—an exact science—that is just as real as the law of gravity.**

It certainly makes a convincing argument to state that the Law of Attraction is a scientifically validated fundamental law of the universe, just as fundamental as the law of gravity. Advocates claim that just as surely as a ball will drop to the ground when you release it from your hand, you cannot fail to get whatever you desire simply by focusing on it. In the words of Wallace Wattles, "There is a science of getting rich, and it is an exact science, like algebra or arithmetic. There are certain laws which govern the process of acquiring riches, and once these laws are learned and obeyed by anyone, that person will get rich with mathematical certainty." And yet, no elaboration is made about those "certain laws"—but instead, he offers a sweeping remark that reads as follows: "…take the conclusions of science as a basis for action, without going into all the processes by which those conclusions were reached."

Much information offered as "scientific" is often distorted. More often than not, only the part of the story that serves the interests of the reporting party is presented, and the facts that don't serve their interests are suppressed.

Such is the case, unfortunately, with much that has been written about the Law of Attraction. In an effort to make it palatable to the general public, its underlying principles of quantum mechanics have been suppressed in favor of highlighting only the principles that can be marketed to the average person who is desperate for self-help solutions. The suppression may have no malice or deliberation intended – it might have even been left out because of the authors', teachers' or producers' ignorance of the intricacies of quantum physics. Nonetheless, the story being told has many gaps that keep the Law of Attraction from being as effective a tool of manifestation as it can be.

The fact remains that **the Law of Attraction is not a physical law**. It cannot even be compared to intangible, invisible things like electricity, microwaves, X-Rays or radio waves because it belongs to the realm of the nonlinear. This fact, however, does not insinuate that it lacks merit. Stating that the Law of Attraction is no less a fundamental law than the law of gravity, or to speak of it in the same breath as physical laws, however, is misleading.

There is an *attempt* to link the Law of Attraction to science by giving the example of the tuning fork. If you hold a tuning fork in your hand and hit its tines against the heel of your hand (i.e., "ding" it), it creates vibrations that move through the air. If you let the tines touch the surface of water, you see ripples, which is the visual evidence of vibration waves. If you ding the tuning fork in a room filled with different kinds of tuning forks calibrated to various pitches, you'll discover that only the tuning forks calibrated to the same frequency as the one you just dinged will vibrate, too. Those who teach the Law of Attraction then conclude that the Law of Attraction is a law of physics that **like forces attract**.

Although the tuning fork certainly makes a stunning and graphic example, it's simply a nice *metaphor* that advocates use to make the "scientific" connection— but it does <u>not</u> represent the true mechanism of how the Law of Attraction works. But it's a convincing metaphor nonetheless.

By calling the Law of Attraction a science, its advocates have actually done themselves a disservice, because this opened the principle up to a heated debate. Even trying to explain the Law of Attraction through the theory of quantum physics is a weak proposition because traditional physicists can argue that signals from subatomic particles (quanta) are imperceptible on the scale of a neuron, let alone a brain or a human being.

What is Quantum Physics?

Simply put, quantum physics is the study of the behavior of atomic and subatomic particles, and their significance in the creation of objects in the dimension of non-time/non-space.

It would be best to categorize the Law of Attraction as an irrefutable spiritual law, rather than a law of physics—one that lies beyond the scope of the provable or the intellect. Any attempts to explain or define it are futile because it resides in the inexplicable, nonmaterial spiritual world. Nonetheless, the Law is so powerful that it is capable of achieving outcomes that are inconceivable in the world of science.

<u>Myth No. 2</u>: **Focus on anything you want to be, do or have—and you shall have that very thing you want to be, do or have.**

The self-help movement and its advocates present the Law of Attraction as a quick fix that takes very little effort. They often claim that all one needs to do is to simply visualize that new car, the dream job, a loving relationship, a great vacation, perfect health, or anything else one wants, and it materializes in no time at all. This is not the case.

In the video, *The Secret*, there was a scene portraying a woman standing in front of a store window, which displayed a beautiful diamond necklace. She gazed upon it with desire in her eyes, and then the film cut to the next scene, wherein she now had the diamond necklace around her neck. We all dream of working that kind of magic, but unfortunately, that's not how the principles behind the Law of Attraction work.

In an interview with *Newsweek*, Fred Alan Wolf, a quantum physicist who was a featured "teacher" in *The Secret*, admits that this one-to-one exchange is not the way manifestation works. He added that it certainly hasn't worked in such a manner in his life.

We all want to entertain the fantasy that if we focused on what we want strongly enough, and imagined it in such intricate detail, what we want will magically materialize in front of our very eyes. Some advocates state that it does require some *action* on our part, and it might take some *time*, but we will eventually have what we want without fail.

If it were only that simple!

Imagine a man using the Law of Attraction to manifest a new Ferrari. He follows the instructions and focuses on the Ferrari in detailed fashion (right down to the feel of the steering wheel in his hands, the sound of the engine, the horsepower, the color of the racing stripes, and all the minute specifications). He even puts a picture of it on the cork board next to his desk at work and thinks about it whenever he can throughout the day. Then, he goes home after a hard day at work— he's in a bad mood so he kicks his dog, yells at his kids and beats his wife.

Will the Law of Attraction manifest his desire for a new Ferrari under these circumstances? No. That's because every thought, action, decision or feeling creates a vortex of interconnected, dynamic energy fields of life

41

that leave a permanent record for all of time. That collective record—and <u>not</u> a singular, focused want or desire—creates the conditions in the quantum field that bring about his circumstances in life. Some call that energy field by other names—the *quantum field*, the spiritual realm, the non-linear domain, the field of all possibilities, the Source of All, Source Energy, the divine intelligence—or its ultimate name, God.

An important thing to remember is that it's never just <u>one</u> thought, action, decision or feeling that brings about <u>one</u> exact outcome. It's the *sum total* of what's recorded in the energy field that manifests everything. Therefore, it's inaccurate to state that focusing one's thoughts on a diamond necklace in the store window will cause that diamond necklace or another one like it to manifest in one's life.

To say that focusing on a car would materialize that car seemingly out of thin air would be doing people a disservice because that's a falsehood. If you've ever heard someone boasting that a car did actually manifest into their lives in this way, it wasn't the Law of Attraction at work but most likely it was *forced* into being through increased risk-taking rather than by some metaphysical effects. I've observed several instances wherein individuals supposedly use the Law of Attraction to manifest their dream car. Then, they later buy their dream car and report that they "attracted" the car into their life, when in actuality, they "forced" themselves to own that car if it's the last thing they did! Oftentimes, what actually happened was that they bought the car even when their financial circumstances hadn't changed by a single penny (perhaps unconsciously to prove that the Law of Attraction does work); they usually don't have a clue as to how to afford the car payments; and hope the Law of Attraction will materialize their car payments. That's not the attraction principle at work.

There's a difference between attraction and inspiration. Almost everyone who has accomplished anything knows that being focused or passionate about achieving a goal or a dream will lead one to move in the same direction as their predominant thoughts. For instance, people might envision themselves as having $100,000 in a savings account, and they consequently *take action* on that picture—by juggling three jobs, budgeting their money, skipping vacations and unnecessary luxuries, etc., eventually saving up the $100,000. That's not the Law of Attraction at work. That's simply inspiration combined with determination.

Attraction, on the other hand, is when people envision themselves as having a particular desired result—and ideal opportunities, people, resources, circumstances, events and situations that contribute to that desired result manifest themselves *without any prompting*. This doesn't mean that action is not necessary because unless people act upon those things that they manifested into their lives, the desired result is not achieved.

The thing to remember is that your positive thoughts are just *one part* of the equation. Your actions, decisions and feelings figure significantly in what's manifested into your life. Collectively, your thoughts, actions, decisions and feelings contribute to the energy field with an infinite number of complex, interacting components, which in turn potentiate an infinite number of possibilities. Even holistic approaches to health are based not just on influencing the protoplasm of the body but, more importantly, the immediate energy field that surrounds, permeates, and governs the condition of the human body.

Myth No. 3: It takes 15 to 17 seconds of pure, focused thought for you to start vibrating on the same frequency as that thought. Those 15 to 17 seconds—uninterrupted by low-vibration thoughts or emotions—are equivalent to 10 hours of activity trying to accomplish what you want.

Law of Attraction advocates sometimes refer to "studies" that supposedly suggest that it takes either 15, 16 or 17 seconds of you focusing on what you want before you begin vibrating. The fact is, thoughts have vibrations that appear the moment the thought enters our mind. Even a split-second thought that emerges below the threshold of one's conscious awareness produces instant vibrations.

To claim that 15 to 17 seconds of pure, focused thought on a desire is equivalent to 10 hours of work towards the accomplishment of that desire is a sweeping generalization that has no basis in fact. No one can make that assertion without taking into consideration the quality and intensity of the *thoughts* and the *work* to which it's being compared. There are obviously countless permutations that would make it difficult to establish a correlation as simplistic as this.

Furthermore, it misleads Law of Attraction practitioners into thinking that with just one 15- to 17-second session of focused thought on one's desire, they're done for the day. After all, a 10-hour workday is more than sufficient for anyone.

This is a falsehood. To expect the manifestation of a desire by just doing 15-17 seconds of pure focused thought a day is like saying one only needs to take a multivitamin capsule once every 5 years and expect it to supply one's nutritional needs for the entire 5 years.

Positive thoughts and feelings mean very little unless you can make it a habit to focus on them frequently throughout the day. Most people can't hold on to high energy feelings, or get themselves to focus on them, for more than just a few seconds or minutes a day. Therefore, the promise of a 15- to 17-second easy "fix" seems like an easy thing to do. Yes, it is easy, but you also can't expect to get any results.

The myth that a 15- to 17-second session is equivalent to 10 hours of work contributes to the risky expectation that one's desires will manifest in record speed. People are generally impatient by nature. When they start practicing the Law of Attraction, most people wait a few days or weeks, and then begin asking themselves, "When is it going to happen?"

When you have such a reaction, it shows that you haven't arrived at the place of trust, wherein your desires are already an eventuality waiting to happen. What you may not realize is that in questioning the status of the manifestation of your desires, you actually slow down the process of their fulfillment because you've allowed your ego to dictate a timeframe. This then means you're setting up *resistance*, instead of just *allowing* the universe (energy field) to bring your desires at the appropriate time.

Another common reaction that slows down manifestation is when you pre-determine *how* your desires will be manifested. Again, this reaction is generated by the ego wanting to control the outcome. If, for example, your desire is to manifest $10,000, your ego "figures out" how it wants you to have it, such as by getting a salary raise, landing a large business deal, winning the lottery, or any of a number of ways. The problem is that your ego has severe limitations—it only knows what is in the scope of your experience or knowledge. It doesn't have access to the myriad possibilities that are beyond your imagination or your concept of what's "real" or "achievable." Therefore, you become attached to the outcome and you look for the evidence you expect to see and may *overlook* the amazing opportunities that the universe delivers. Again, this is a form of resistance to the flow of the universe. It's like putting a huge boulder in the middle of a rushing river—and slowing down the speed by which the manifestation of your desires arrives at your banks.

Don't Resist the Flow

There's a story about a group of Chinese men walking through the woods beside a rushing river. Suddenly, they spotted the body of an old man bobbing up and down in the roaring rapids. Thinking the old man was dead, they ran to the river's edge trying to figure out how they were going to fish the body out of the water so that it wouldn't be swept out to sea. Their discussion came to an abrupt halt when the old man, who they had thought was dead, emerged out of the water, dried himself off and started walking away. The men ran after the old man and asked, "How did you survive in that water? No one could swim in that water without being killed." "It is really easy," the old man replied. "I just went up when the water went up, and down when the water went down."

Myth No. 4: **When something bad happens to you—tragedy, misfortune, illness, disaster and all their expressions—you attracted it to yourself by your own negative thoughts that you send out into the universe, whether you're aware of it or not.**

While there is *some* truth to the above statement, its full mechanics are not as simple as represented by the current teaching of the Law of Attraction. One only needs to look at the tragic things that sometimes happen to innocent young children to know that the children did not bring the tragedy upon themselves. Or one could look at the fate of those who perished in the South Asian tsunami, the Gulf War, the World Trade Center, or Hurricane Katrina and know that those people did not bring their deaths upon themselves, no matter what religious zealots say.

It would take volumes to explain the ramifications of genetic predisposition, collective consciousness, karma and a host of other factors that play a role in bringing about events, circumstances, situations and conditions in life. One cannot fully discuss those without being prepared to delve into controversial subjects such as why people are born into specific circumstances, geographic locations, and social strata. One must accept the fact that bad things cannot be simplistically explained as things that people attracted to themselves.

There's a danger in propagating this myth (or what I would call a partial truth), and it is this: When bad things do happen, a person is likely to blame himself (or herself) for attracting the bad thing. Their mind perceives that the negative circumstances—such as getting into an accident, the death of a loved one, getting fired from their job, illness, or even small things like a stopped up sink or finding no parking space—are their fault, and they attracted those circumstances through the thoughts and feelings they've had in this lifetime and in this dimension. They then react with feelings of inadequacy, guilt, frustration, failure, fear or denial—and they project those internal emotions upon the world.

Suffice it to say, therefore, that *some* bad things do happen as a consequence of you vibrationally attracting such things to yourself through the negative thoughts and feelings you emit. The majority of bad things, however, are *karmically propelled*—that is, they are due to one or more of the unlimited combinations of thoughts, feelings, decisions, actions and other factors (not only *yours* but also those of *others*), contributing to the energy field, which in turn brings about events, circumstances, conditions and situations.

Much as we, as human beings, are inclined to put labels on all things, or impose our theories about what causes what, there is no exact science for figuring out exactly what combination of factors causes a particular thing to happen to a person or a group of persons at a given time or place. Release yourself from self-blame when something bad happens to you. Don't fault yourself for it because more often than not, you had no *direct influence* on the outcome any more than the victims of Hurricane Katrina consciously (or unconsciously) attracted the disaster to themselves. The best thing to do is to let go of all experiences that you perceive to be undesirable or unfortunate, and trust instead

51

in the higher providential (karmic) order of things. Know that good things happen through the good thoughts, feelings, decisions and actions that you sow into the energy field. In the next chapter, you will discover the single most powerful thing you can sow in that field that results in all good things.

Myth No. 5: In order to attract what you want, you must focus your attention on what you want.

This Law of Attraction "rule" probably came about to differentiate the fact that one must not focus on what one does not want (such as debt, grief, heartbreak, weight problems, financial problems and other "normal" things that people unconsciously focus on)— but instead focus on what one wants.

While focusing on what you want is infinitely better than focusing on what you don't want, the higher truth is that in order to get what you want in life you have to *let go of wanting it in the first place.* This is probably the most important distinction between the current teaching on the Law of Attraction and the greatest manifestation principle that will become clear to you as you continue reading this book. This point of departure is also probably the most difficult to accept and adopt because it *seems* to go against the principles of positive thinking and the traditional procedure for manifesting desires.

However, when you fully understand and embrace the principle of letting go of desires, that's when you'll truly begin to manifest them consistently. When you're willing to surrender your desire to the divine, what you get is infinitely better than what you desired in the first place.

Here's how the process of desire works:

The moment you create a desire in your mind, you create its opposite at that very instant. This is called the positionality of duality. In plain English, what this means is when you take a position about something—anything—such as "I intend to be rich," its polar opposite (in this case, poverty or lack of wealth), necessarily has to appear because of the inherent duality of all thought. You cannot perceive wealth except against the background of poverty (or the absence of wealth), nor can you perceive happiness except against the background of unhappiness. Every position that you take exists only relative to its opposite. In Chinese philosophy, this is called the yin and yang principle—the two opposing forces in the universe.

Consider this: How would you know something is noisy if you don't have its opposite—silence—against which to define it? Likewise, you can't perceive darkness except as the absence of light, and one can't really know joy unless you understand the concept of sadness or sorrow.

Furthermore, when you desire or want to have something in your life, say, a million dollars, it reinforces the reality that you don't have a million dollars. "Wanting" things reinforces a state of *lack* and keeps you in a state of *wanting*. Focusing on this brings you more lack.

Contrary to popular belief, it's <u>not</u> your mental focus that causes your desires to happen—but rather, it is **how well you connect to, or how much you are in harmony with, the energy field which is responsible for all of creation**. Everything you are, including your emotions, feelings, beliefs and prayers in every moment represents your ongoing communication with the energy field. And the circumstances in your life are the energy field's response to your communication.

That is why the Law of Attraction *seems* to work in an erratic hit-or-miss fashion. It seems to work for some people but not for others. It seems to work under certain conditions and not in others. Actually, it works all the time—but not in the way you've been taught.

You already *know* at the deepest level of your being what you desire—and there's no need to *focus* on it. You simply connect to the energy field, which is God, and *allow* your heart's desires to manifest. In some spiritual traditions, this is explained thus: Those who seek God shall lack no good thing.

This then is the essence of co-creation. Your ego may delude you into thinking that your thought vibrations are manifesting or creating your desired outcomes. The truth is that you never do the creating yourself. It's always a co-creation with God, with the universe, with the Source of All, with the energy field that quantum physicists call the quantum field.

All that's required of you is that you transcend your ego and just allow the energy field to bring you what your heart desires. God already knows what you want even before you ask—you just have to learn how to reconnect to the energy field so that you can tap into the immense creative power of the field. Let go of the state of "wanting" and be in the state of "having" or "accepting" instead. The energy field encompasses all things; therefore, it also encompasses everything that you find lacking in your life. When you fully embrace the truth that you are inextricably connected to this energy field, and that you're not a separate entity fending for yourself in the vast frontier of the cosmos, you will begin to realize that you're already connected with everything you want.

Instead of focusing on your desire, a better strategy would be to hold in mind that which you desire <u>without</u> adding desire to it. This means that you can picture yourself living in abundant wealth, for instance, but detach yourself from the state of wanting wealth. That way, there's no positionality—i.e., you're not taking a position. You're simply envisioning something that's already real in the energy field.

You must come from the elevated standpoint of being connected to the energy field (God). In this way, you invite your desire to transform itself from the unmanifest (formless potential) to the manifest. If you operate from the ego, however, your ego will come up with a host of objections to prove that what you're envisioning is not true.

This may seem like mere semantics to you, but the truth remains that we live in a semantic universe and our reality is molded by language. The language we use in our everyday lives puts us in either empowering or disempowering states—sometimes without our knowing it—and whenever we can, we must choose language that empowers us.

Even the semantics, however, are eclipsed by the deep and profound spiritual truth about what truly causes everything we want to happen in our lives. This truth is not—nor has ever been—a secret. It is something that has been available to all since the beginning of time—something held sacred and taught in all the major spiritual traditions, as well as all the spiritual books, including the Bible. The only thing that has been a secret is that people haven't known—until now —that this spiritual truth is the greatest manifestation principle in the world, and is the missing ingredient that makes the Law of Attraction powerful.

In fact, whenever the Law of Attraction has been

shown to work, more often than not, it is this principle that caused it to work. And this principle is the subject of the next chapter.

.

Chapter 4

To Love is to Live

*C*ritics often deplore the materialistic ideals that the practice of the Law of Attraction propagates. That's because most people, upon learning the manifestation promises of the Law of Attraction, are drawn almost magnetically into the realm of materialism. They gravitate to self-centered acquisitions such as houses, cars, jewelry and vacations. As reported in *Newsweek* magazine, even some of the participants in the video, *The Secret*, expressed dismay over the "relentless materialism" portrayed in the film. Two of the speakers featured in the documentary reportedly expressed concern that the film might make the process of manifestation seem magical, which it is not. That was undoubtedly a reaction to the film's depiction of the Law of Attraction as being like Aladdin's genie that grants our every command.

One important thing to bear in mind is that it is <u>never</u> materialism or the desire for personal gain that manifests your desires. Therefore, for as long as your desires are motivated by materialism, personal gain or other selfish interests, you can visualize your desires all day long and yet you may never get what you want. One might argue that there are people and corporate entities that have acquired millions by operating from selfish and sometimes even downright ruthless and unscrupulous principles. Perhaps what one should consider are the multimillions those people and companies *don't* make because they espouse selfish interests.

In practicing the Law of Attraction, while it's possible to observe good things happening in your life, more often than not, it is either *confirmation bias* or the *observer-expectancy effect* that may be causing you to observe those good things. Confirmation bias, in the context of psychology and cognitive science, is one's tendency to search for or interpret new information in a way that confirms one's preconceived beliefs, and

ignore information and interpretations which contra-
dict such preconceived beliefs.

The observer-expectancy effect (also called the
experimenter effect) is a similar bias found in scientific
research when a researcher expects a given result, and
therefore unconsciously manipulates an experiment in
order to find that result. To eliminate that effect in
clinical studies, the double-blind methodology is often
used.

In the practice of the Law of Attraction, you're
directed to expect good things to happen to you as a
result of positive, high-frequency thoughts. When you
do this, your level of alertness is raised so that when
events do occur (that may or may not have anything to
do with the attraction principle), you not only notice
them—you *magnify* them, and point to them as
evidence that the Law of Attraction works.

For instance, I personally know some Law of
Attraction practitioners who enjoy pointing to the fact
that they get ideal parking spaces at shopping malls or
other places where good parking spaces are hard to
find. They insist that's the Law of Attraction at work.
This begs the question: Wouldn't they have snagged

those parking spaces anyway whether they had practiced the Law of Attraction or not? Isn't it a fact that they just noticed their "good fortune" of finding the parking spots because they were *looking* for evidence that the Law of Attraction works? And more importantly, how many times do they get good parking spaces as compared to the number of times they get lousy (or no) parking spaces in any given week, month or year? That's the acid test. Invariably, the answer is somewhere along the lines of 1 in 10 to 1 in 5.

Therefore, that's about a 10% to 20% batting average. Is that anything to get excited about, or does it state conclusively that the Law of Attraction works? I think not.

So what does work? There is a powerful manifestation principle, which, when applied to the Law of Attraction dramatically increases the likelihood that your desires will materialize. Let me tell you about some studies that will illustrate this powerful principle.

Research has been conducted in recent years to shed some light on **spectacular athletic achievements**. What causes an athlete to excel in an athletic event, and even break through a performance barrier to a new level of human possibility? Proceeding from the proven axiom that the human body becomes stronger or weaker depending on one's mental state, researchers asked the test athletes to hold in mind either positive or negative *motives* for wanting to win the athletic event they were about to enter—and they then measured the athletes' muscle strength using a clinical kinesiological muscle testing method that has been used as a diagnostic technique and verified widely over the past 25 years. The researchers discovered that when the athlete held in mind selfish motives for winning, such as the hope of becoming a star, making a lot of money, or defeating his opponent, the muscle tested weak. But when the athlete held in mind noble motives such as the dedication of his performance to someone he loves, the honor of his country or his sport, or the joy of exerting maximum effort for the sake of excellence, the muscle tested powerfully strong! It was concluded that when athletes are awash in the belief that their excellence goes beyond personal ambition and accomplishment, and that it's a gift to mankind as a demonstration of man's potential, their bodies go strong and remain strong throughout a competitive event, often transcending ordinary human limitations.

Research has also been done to shed some light on the **miracle of spontaneous recovery from illness**. What causes a person who is suffering from an incurable, and often lingering, disease or sickness to be healed spontaneously and restored to perfect health, usually without any medical intervention? It was discovered that frequently, there was a significant increase in the sick person's *capacity to love*, accompanied by the *awareness of the importance of love* as a healing factor.

Conversely, it has been observed that in those whose disease progressed rapidly, there was a marked increase in fear (which is the contrarian opposite of love), as well as anxiety, doubt, depression and stress.

Incidentally, the California woman named Sylvia (mentioned in Chapter 1), who had suffered from Stage 4 lymphoma, reported that prior to receiving her cancer diagnosis, she had felt *unloved* for a long time. She had feared her marriage was on the rocks and that her husband was not supportive of her; she endured tremendous discord with her in-laws; and her marriage eventually ended in a hostile divorce. Her oncologist, who is also the head of one of the most prestigious cancer centers in the country, a medical professional who normally deals only in hard science, had the wisdom to tell Sylvia about recognizing the importance of love in her healing. She ended every visit with Sylvia with the words, "I love you"—words that are seldom said by a doctor to a patient. Sylvia believes that her doctor was the catalyst that enabled her to allow love to become the central focus of her healing, and eventually freed her from cancer.

Masaru Emoto, a creative and visionary Japanese researcher, observed that water reacts to different environmental conditions, music and even pollution. This led him and his colleagues to conduct experiments to see how thoughts and words affect water. They used specific words typed on a word processor and printed onto paper, and taped the paper on glass bottles containing untreated, distilled water overnight. They then froze the waters and photographed the molecules using a special microscopic camera. They found that the words caused the formation of either crystalline structures or distorted shapes, depending on the meaning or sentiment conveyed by the words.

The word "love" had a beautifully formed snowflake-like geometric design in a crystalline structure while the word "hate" had distorted and randomly formed crystalline structures. One interesting observation is that the name of Mother Teresa, the late humanitarian, who was beatified and who some say was the most loving person in the world, formed a beautiful crystalline structure similar to the one formed by the word "love." The crystalline structures formed by classical versus heavy metal music, positive emotions versus negative emotions, and people who exuded love versus those who exuded hatred and megalomania (Adolf Hitler) are quite revealing. They indicate that water is highly responsive to our thoughts, words and emotions. Since water comprises over 70% of the average adult human body, it could be surmised that we can heal and transform our lives with the thoughts we surround ourselves with. More importantly, the study reveals that in the hierarchy of emotions, love (followed by gratitude) is the supreme transformation catalyst of all.

I am certain it has become clear to you that the recurring theme in the above findings is *love*. What is love—and what role does it play in the Law of Attraction and the manifestation of our desires?

Love is a state of being not a state of *feeling*. It goes well beyond the realm of the emotions. It's an attitude of benevolence and kindness towards all creation, including one's self, at all times and under all circumstances.

Love is the most powerful magnetic force in the universe. It is the doorway from the unmanifest to the manifest, and the bridge between the emotional and the spiritual—the pathway from the linear to the nonlinear domains. Love is the dynamic force by which the perfection of the physical world was created. Any endeavor that employs the magnetism of love MUST necessarily manifest because love's frequency is a vibrational match to that of God, who is the architect of all creation.

When you consider that superior athletes are able to break through barriers of human possibility when motivated by love, so can *you* break through to the unimaginable, indescribable world where effortless creation is a way of life.

The Greatest Manifestation Principle in the World

Love is the catalyst by which all good things happen. The effortless way to achieve your heart's desire is to let go of your attachment to results, and focus on love instead. Bring the power of love to your pursuits and to all the people, relationships, resources and events associated with your pursuits. The outcome you get may be different from what you had in mind, but it will be infinitely better than that which you desired.

From the time we're old enough to talk, our parents, society, and the world in general, train us to be results-oriented. We measure our success—and oftentimes our worth—by the results produced by our efforts. Therefore, the majority of us form the lifelong habit of focusing on the results we want—and fail to activate the one thing—love—that gives wings to our desires.

That's because we subscribe to the belief that our actions cause results. We do a specific task and we get a specific result. We study hard—and we pass the exam. We send out resumes and go on job interviews—and we get a job. We build a better mousetrap—and the world beats a path to our door. We act, look and behave a certain way, and we attract the attention of the opposite sex. And by extension, we focus on our desires in an effort to trigger the Law of Attraction and attract to ourselves the things we want in life.

When your desire is *motivated* by love—and *nourished* by love—it has the highest likelihood of manifestation. In the process of co-creation, love is the single most valuable thing you can contribute that is in harmony with all that is.

How to Use the Greatest Manifestation Principle to Manifest Your Desires

Step 1: Think about the desires you have at present. Are they motivated by love—or by selfish interests, ambition, revenge, personal gain, or other things? If they are motivated by anything other than love, refine your desire in a way that it becomes an expression of love—perhaps one that is of benefit not just to you, but to others or mankind.

Step 2: Now, think about how you go about the pursuit of your desire. Do you nourish every aspect of your pursuit with love—or do you operate from a spirit of hostile competition, one-upmanship, wrongful pride, exploitation of the weak, shrewdness, control-freakishness or other things? If you're surrounding the pursuit of your desire with anything other than love, change your actions and attitudes to embrace a benevolence and kindness towards everyone you encounter. Think of what you can do to make other people's lives more joyful instead of focusing on their usefulness to you. Think of ways of expanding the scope of your pursuit to benefit more people and be of service to mankind. When you encounter conflict or problems, let go of your need to control every situation, your need to win every argument or your need to appear superior. In every transaction, whether business or personal, ask yourself the question, *'How can I bring love to this interaction?'*

Step 3: Stay connected to the energy field (which is responsible for all of creation, including manifestation) by being in a state of love as often as possible throughout the day. The best way to do this is by practicing the *Love's Pathway* exercise described in Chapter 5, one or more times a day. Whenever you're experiencing the low-energy states of fear, stress, doubt, worry, sadness, anger, frustration, apathy, grief, guilt or shame, do the "flip-switch" maneuver by saying the following abbreviated version of *Love's Pathway* to yourself: *I am the full expression of God's love. Just as God is love, so am I. I am love.* You may also say it to yourself any time throughout the day. When the high-frequency vibration of love occupies the same field as lower energies, the lower energies are nullified and converted to higher energies.

It is important to emphasize that "connecting to the energy field" does not presuppose that you are not a part of the energy field. You are in the field—and it is in you. The only thing that keeps you separate from it, from being one with it, is your identification with your ego. The energy field is not some nebulous, vaporous mass located somewhere outside of you, but rather it is the *totality of creation*, both visible and invisible. Therefore, there is no place you can go, and no step you can take anywhere without being in it. It envelops and enfolds you, and when you shed your ego consciousness, you merge with it. Think of an egg yolk suspended in the albumen (egg white). There is a membrane around the yolk which keeps the yolk separate from the albumen. When you puncture the membrane, the yolk unites with the albumen. The same is true with you—when you take your ego out of the equation, you dissolve into a oneness with the field. When you say the abbreviated version of Love's Pathway above ("I am the full expression of God's love...") or practice the Love's Pathway exercise, you train yourself to become aware that the field (God) and you are one.

Think for a moment how your life might change when you follow the 3 steps suggested above. Observe how quickly your desires will manifest when you're in harmony with the universe instead of resisting the natural flow, and separating yourself from others and the world. Notice how joyful the people around you will be and how they will be inclined to contribute to the fulfillment of your desires. Think about how your stress levels will be reduced to a minimum (or to nothing). Imagine how love can enable you to enjoy your life now instead of living for some hoped-for bounty in the uncertain future.

For comparison purposes, consider the above 3-step scenario of manifesting versus the typical way people practice the Law of Attraction (below): ⬇

You have a desire—and you're excited to use the Law of Attraction to manifest it. Chances are, your desire is motivated by personal gain, materialism or some other self-centered pursuit. If your desire happens to be a tangible thing, you cut out a picture of the thing you desire from a magazine or brochure, and you tape it on your bathroom mirror, or wherever you can see it everyday. You visualize your desire often throughout the day. The more you focus on it, the more self-absorbed and emotionally attached you become. Every day, every week and every month that passes by when you don't manifest your desire is a reminder of your failure. You don't enjoy the process of being without the thing you desire, so you fantasize about some mind-projected future when you hope you will get what you want. After you've given daily visualization a fair try and your desire still hasn't manifested, you gradually drop out of the practice. You used to focus on your wants everyday, but you cut down to 5 days a week, then 3, then 1, then none. You conclude that the Law of Attraction doesn't work, but you feel it was a personal failure—and the failure weighs heavily on you. People around you feel your low energy and you attract more of it, sending you into a downward spiral. The failure not only debilitates you, but you're also still without that thing you desire.

Which of the two ways of manifesting described above feels right to you?

I've tried both ways—and the difference is like night and day. Whenever my desire was motivated and nourished by love, I usually manifest not just one but multiple desirable occurrences or opportunities in a relatively short period of time. Two of my experiences are particularly memorable. The first one happened in 2004. I had just finished writing the manuscript of a novel, and it was in dire need of editing. I searched on the Internet for a talented editor who writes in a style similar to mine. I was unable to find one who was suitable, and who could work within my timeline. Meanwhile, I met a woman who had bought my first book (a business book). She was interested in purchasing my advanced CD course but didn't have the $300 to pay for it. I decided to send her the CD course for free and even offered her complimentary access to my personal mentoring program, which normally costs $900. She was so grateful, and she insisted on doing something to repay me for what I had done for her. I told her I didn't require any remuneration or reciprocation of any kind. A few weeks later, in a phone conversation, I happened to mention to her that I had written a novel. That sparked her interest because it turned out, she was a professional novel editor! As evidence of the manifestation principle at work, she offered to edit my novel—and refused to accept any payment from me. She was the perfect editor for my novel, and her writing style harmonized well with mine. The best part was that her offer to edit my novel came at a time in my career when I was able to devote time to work on the edits with her. Four months later, with her expert help, I finished the novel—and it is presently enjoying commercial success and receiving wonderful praise from readers all over the world (Note: This is a pseudonymous work). I'm constantly amazed at what a little loving kindness can do.

The above example illustrates clearly that love is not just something you can apply towards the manifestation of your desires. Whenever you exercise love and kindness towards others—even when it has nothing to do with your desires—the universe has a way of rewarding you by looking after your needs. Notice, too, that I was not focusing on the desire to finalize my novel and get it published, but instead I had let go of the desire, trusting that the universe would provide what I desired. And sure enough, it came. Another point worthy of note is that the novel I wrote was a labor of love, one that I knew was accomplished only with the help of the Greater Hand. I self-published it not with the intention of enriching myself but to enlighten readers with the deep spiritual insights contained therein. I believe my motivation to serve mankind is the reason the novel is so well-received. Earlier on, I mentioned that this scenario generated multiple manifestations. It was amazing how service providers, vendors and other resources seemed to appear out of nowhere to handle the publishing and marketing details.

When you live your life from the standpoint of being of benefit or service to others or mankind (instead of selfish interests), or operate from the premise of supporting life and all creation, the universe will respond with ways to benefit and support you.

Mark Victor Hansen, who co-authored the *Chicken Soup for the Soul* series of books, which has sold over 100 million copies, is someone whose success can also find its roots in the greatest manifestation principle in the world. He operates from the standpoint that *money is never the ultimate goal.* The original *Chicken Soup for the Soul* book (which he co-authored with Jack Canfield) was a gift to mankind. The stories in the book provide inspiration and hope to millions of people throughout the world. It's important to note that the publishing rights were initially offered to 134 publishers, but no one wanted to publish the book. But the greatest manifestation principle was at work, and one little publisher in Deerfield, Florida, picked up the publishing rights. The rest, as they say, is history—and the *Chicken Soup for the Soul* series now has over 100 titles and counting. But it doesn't end there. Instead of hoarding away the money his writing has afforded him, Mark has given away millions of dollars to various charities. He has even co-founded an "enlightened wealth" organization which helps members reach their financial goals, and thereafter, share their wealth by donating cash to charitable organizations or by performing hours of community service. The goal is to inspire a million millionaires—and as of the time of this writing, the organization members have given away $30,625,780 in donations, and performed 324,367 hours of community service. Is it any wonder that Mark is one of the wealthiest and most successful authors and entrepreneurs around?

Here's another example of how the greatest manifestation principle in the world has worked for me in a most *unexpected* way. I entered into a business partnership with someone I barely knew because of promises he made that seemed attractive to me. It turned out that he could not deliver on many things that he said he could do for me. I gave him all the chances in the world, and tried to be patient. Five months went by and still nothing. I was terribly disappointed at first but decided that the low energy wasn't going to do anyone any good. So I decided to shower him with the kind of love and appreciation one would accord a worthy business partner. He was startled by my behavior, and didn't know what to say. I know he felt secretly relieved that I wasn't upset, and he must have appreciated the kindness I showed him despite his inability to deliver on any of his promises. Nothing ever came of that business partnership, but something miraculous did happen that I know was a direct result of the greatest manifestation principle I had practiced on the ill-fated business partnership. Right around the time that the partnership was dissolving, a friend of mine introduced me to a woman—and that woman presented me with a business deal that ended up being multiple times more lucrative than I expected the failed business partnership to be.

The above example illustrates yet again that love's rewards are beyond comprehension, and are usually much more than one had hoped for or imagined. It also goes to show that sometimes it isn't always what you focus on that will yield the fulfillment of your desires. Sometimes, the rewards come from the most unexpected sources. This is true, too, when it comes to people who are the recipients of your love and kindness —they will not necessarily be the ones to reciprocate or reward you. Acts of love and kindness have no boundaries, and their rewards often don't come from where you expect them to originate.

It should be noted that the concept of love, as presented here, is a way for you to **be**—as opposed to merely a way for you to act, look or behave. When you give full expression to your loving nature, people around you will also be positively influenced to give full expression to their loving nature towards you—not through your prompting but as a consequence of being in your vicinity. You attract to yourself that which you emanate. When you remove the obstacles to the awareness of love's presence within you, it becomes easy to love yourself and others as well. When you love yourself, you project that love upon the world. The more you love yourself, the more loving your world becomes—and you begin to experience a world of your own creation.

> "We don't see things as <u>they</u> are.
> We see them as <u>we</u> are."
> —Anaïs Nin

In the first of two *Oprah* shows featuring the "teachers" in the video, *The Secret*, Oprah Winfrey mentioned that she had been practicing the principles of the Law of Attraction all her life, but she didn't know it was a *secret*. She was right. The Law of Attraction is neither a new concept, nor was it ever a secret. It's something that has been known and taught for thousands of years by early mystical Christians, Hindus, Babylonians, Taoists and others. In truth, Oprah's undeniable success and fulfillment in life has more to do with her faithful practice of the most powerful manifestation principle in the world (love) than it does about focusing on positive thoughts or feelings. I believe that her love for people, and her desire for people to live their best lives—<u>not</u> her constant focus on her own desires—is what made her one of the richest and influential people in the world. No matter what anyone's personal opinions or feelings may be about Oprah, most people respect her. She's a positive force in the media, she covers numerous topics that other talk shows wouldn't dare to attempt, she continually delivers spiritually uplifting messages, helps people find meaning in their lives, and uses her influence, fame and finances to be of service to humanity whenever she can.

Another person who lived by the principle of love, and went on to become one of the most successful people in the world was the late Sam Walton, the founder of the most successful retail chain in the world. Again, whatever anyone's personal opinions or feelings may be about him, and no matter what heat Wal-Mart may have received in recent years, one can't help but admire Sam and what he has accomplished while he was alive. He was a business person who was so often imitated—and yet no retail company has ever managed to duplicate his success. Because unbeknownst to the public, who saw only Sam's business acuity, marketing genius, and his ability to efficiently manage a gigantic business enterprise, Sam had love at the heart of his operations. During Sam's lifetime, Wal-Mart was a company that was reputed to have "heart" just as its founder, Sam, had "heart." He loved his customers, his employees and people in general. Customer goodwill was the driving force of his empire. He also nurtured and supported his employees, and made them feel that they were an important part of the Wal-Mart family. He trained them to be committed to service, to the support of life and human value. It's no wonder Sam attained the success he did.

Love is—and has always been—the most powerful currency of the world. Yet, only a small percentage of people in this world live by the principle of love. All the great spiritual leaders of the world have embraced this principle and called it "the way" to ultimate fulfillment.

Instead, the majority of us still live our lives without using this principle. Interestingly enough, the fields of psychology, mental health and other self-improvement disciplines often advise us to do the opposite of this greatest manifestation principle in the world—advocating the focus on results instead of love.

While there's nothing intrinsically wrong with focusing on the things you want in life—and getting your desires so clear that you can almost see them, smell them, hear, touch and feel them—the present teachings on the Law of Attraction fail to mention what it is that takes those desires from their unformed potentiality to physical actuality—and that is, love.

Visualizing and affirming your desires without adding love to the equation is akin to a rocket that doesn't have sufficient propulsion to catapult it into space.

I've no doubt the people who have managed to succeed by focusing on their desires must have unwittingly fueled their intentions with love somewhere along the way. If they didn't put love in the equation and still managed to make a fortune, one has to wonder how much larger a fortune they might have made if they did focus on love.

The same holds true when it comes to relationships. Some couples manage to make their relationship work by going through the motions—and even when they're driven by selfish motives and not by love. But one has to wonder how much more blissful their relationship could be if they made love the focus of their relationship.

Not All Positive Thoughts Are Created Equal

If you're like most people who practice the Law of Attraction, the first thing you learned was that thinking positive thoughts is the best way to attract positive things that are a vibrational match to your thoughts. You've been taught to acquire the habit of thinking of thoughts that make you feel good, and replacing a negative thought with a positive thought (flip-switching) the moment you sense a negative thought arising. The positive thought could be anything from picturing a giggling baby, to visualizing yourself enjoying a vacation at your favorite destination, to feeling the exhilaration of seeing a rainbow after a storm—or anything that gives you those warm, fuzzy feelings.

One thing I noticed is that most people don't make any differentiation between the positive thoughts or feelings they generate—seldom favoring one over another, and usually using whatever thought or feeling is easiest to manufacture at will. Sometimes, for variety, people even mix up the positive thoughts—or rotate all of them just to cover all the bases. But in so doing, they often pay little attention to—or ignore altogether—the *one* positive thought (love) that really makes the big difference.

Ultimately, the results they get are usually diluted—either they manifest their desires sporadically with no consistency whatsoever, or they don't manifest their desires at all. Is it any wonder why those who practice the Law of Attraction get more misses than hits as far as the manifestation of their desires go?

You see, positive thoughts and feelings are not all created equal. Just thinking of something pleasurable or delightful creates vibrations of a lower frequency than love because those thoughts and feelings are self-oriented (receiving) whereas love is outwardly-oriented (giving). Consider the athletes mentioned in the beginning of this chapter. When they held in mind selfish motives for winning—even when that motive was accompanied by positive thoughts of becoming a star or making a lot of money, they tested weak in the muscle test. When they held in mind noble motives such as the dedication of their performance to someone they love or for the love of their country, or viewed their athletic performance as a gift to mankind, they tested strong, excelled in athletic events, and sometimes even broke through a performance barrier to a new level of human possibility.

One might conclude that giving, not getting, is the key to true achievement and the manifestation of desires. This is not to say that people have never been known to achieve things through selfish ambition. Yes, they have. However, rarely does achievement derived from selfish aims ever produce an enduring sense of accomplishment and joy.

Suffice it to say, therefore, that in the pursuit of your desires, ascend to the level of love before choosing any other positive thoughts and feelings. Love has the vibrational power against which all other positive thoughts and feelings pale by comparison.

The Undercurrent of All Your Activities

As previously mentioned, it is possible to generate some results by being results-oriented instead of focusing on love. However, it's worthwhile to ask the question: *What results are you _not_ getting* because you didn't apply the greatest success principle in the pursuit of your goals?

When you switch your focus to love instead of desires, and allow love to be the undercurrent of all your activities …

… you will free yourself from past concerns and wasteful preoccupations

… your creativity becomes fully expressed

… you gain a charisma to which people are magnetically drawn

… your entire outlook on life and relationships will improve

… you will gain excellence in any field of human endeavor that you choose

… you will spontaneously attract people who are like-minded and who will be instrumental in the fulfillment of your desires

… you will be able to easily let go of the non-essential and deleterious things in your life; and

… you will raise the energy level of anyone in your vicinity.

> "If you gain the world and all its bounty,
> but have no love, your life is but a dance
> without a soul, a song without a heart,
> or a prayer without devotion."
> —Carnelian Sage

A desire that is motivated by a higher principle, such as love, peace, loyalty, dedication to God, truth or country is a desire whose manifestation brings great spiritual upliftment. The greatest of those higher principles is love. Those who acquire things in their life through the use of force, or by operating from anything other than love or other life-enhancing principles, get results that have no spiritual merit—and the pleasure derived from them is short-lived like the high derived from a drug.

Knowing this, how might your life change if instead of focusing on worldly pursuits that are ephemeral, transient and corruptible, you began focusing on love, which has eternal value?

Consider the life of Mother Teresa. According to the Gallup poll, she was the single most widely admired person of the 20th century. She wielded great influence on those around her not only by virtue of her humanitarian and charitable work among the poverty-stricken people of India and the world, but because of the energy field of love that surrounded her. It has been said that while Mother Teresa was living, whenever she entered a roomful of people, every person would sense her loving presence even if they didn't see her step into the room.

Mother Teresa inspired countless people all over the world, and her love has had an indescribable effect on people. Oscar-nominated Spanish actress, Penelope Cruz, for instance, spent a week doing volunteer work for Mother Teresa in 1997, which included assisting in a leprosy clinic in Calcutta. Penelope reportedly said in an interview, "To spend a week with Mother Teresa? I was more excited to do that than to get the greatest movie. When you are with her, you feel more useful than at any time in your life." The year after Penelope's visit to Calcutta, she landed her first starring role in an English-language film, *The Hi-Lo Country*—and Penelope donated her entire salary from the film to Mother Teresa's charity. Her trip to India inspired her so much that she helped start a foundation to support homeless girls in India. One might ask the question: Could it be that it is Penelope's use of the greatest manifestation principle in the world that brought about the kind of success she's had in both American and Spanish cinema in the last decade?

> "It is not how much you do, but how much love you put into the doing that matters."
> —Mother Teresa

A sequoia seed in your hand has the potential to become a Giant Sequoia tree. But it's not a Giant Sequoia tree yet. It's only a seed in your hand. You cannot cause it to become a Giant Sequoia tree, even if you spent your whole life visualizing that it is a Giant Sequoia tree. But what you can do is provide the *conditions* in which the seed's potentiality comes into manifestation. Just add fertile soil, sunshine and rain— and just like clockwork it will grow into a giant tree, perhaps reaching a height of 350 to 400 feet like some of the tallest Sequoias in the world. The seed becomes a tree because of the creative power of the energy field that allows the seed's unformed potential to manifest into actuality. Likewise, your desire is much like a seed in your hand. You cannot cause it to transform itself from a desire to the actualization of that desire unless you provide the *conditions* in which its potentiality comes into manifestation. The major condition necessary for that to happen is love. Other conditions, such as the positive thoughts, feelings and visualization do help, but the actualization of your desire will be stunted and will never grow to the highest of its potential without love. Therefore, nourish your desire with love and imbue everything around it with the power of devotion.

Although love is the most powerful ingredient for manifesting desires, it is hoped that this application of it does not become a mere means to an end. Instead, endeavor to love because you *want* to love—because it is the full expression of God in you. You must love because you *get* to love—it is a privilege, not an obligation. And finally, love because you can never be more like God than when you love other human beings for love's own sake.

To love is to live.

 Chapter 5

Entering the Realm of Miracles

> Miracles occur naturally as expressions of
> love. The real miracle is the love that
> inspires them. In this sense everything that
> comes from love is a miracle.
>
> —Excerpt from <u>A Course in Miracles</u>

*L*ove is not just something you do. It's what you are.

Most people live their lives in a state of oblivious slumber, never awakening to the realization of this spiritual truth.

As explained in the previous chapter, love is the attitude of benevolence, reverence and kindness for all creation, including one's self, at all times and under all circumstances.

Every man, woman and child has love at the core of their being. It's every person's natural inheritance. If you subscribe to the premise that you are made in the image and likeness of God, then just as God is love, so are you. And so is every human being in the world.

Contrary to what most people might think, and what Webster's dictionary says, love is not an emotion or a feeling. Neither is it a commodity that you give to another human being or receive from another human being. Neither is it something that you can create or extinguish. Rather, love is the essence of who you are. It is something you embody as a human being. More than the flesh and bones that comprise your body, more than the blood coursing through your veins, and more than the 6,000 miles of neurons wired throughout your body, you are—first and foremost—love.

I often compare a human being to a computer. The person's essential nature, which is love, is the computer hardware. This hardware never changes, no matter what software runs on it. The programs that are installed in that hardware by society, upbringing, education, experience and everything else are the software. The software is what's running in the forefront, and the computer begins to be identified with the programs it runs (what it can *do*) and not its hardware (what it *is*). But the nature of the hardware is not affected—it just runs quietly in the background.

It's the same thing with human beings. Love is their true nature—but because they're programmed by the things of the world, you only see what they *do* and not who they *are*.

A human being's nature (love) remains unblemished, no matter what behavior they display—no matter what actions they take, what thoughts they think or what words they speak. They still remain as love in disguise.

Knowing this, it should become easier for you to discern the inherent beauty that resides within each person. When they hurt you, offend you and take advantage of you, you'll know that it's a result of the programs they're running and you're able to perceive them from a place of compassion, and forgive them for they're unaware that they're acting unconsciously, oblivious of their true nature.

At some point, a computer could be corrupted by the programs that are running on it, or by other extraneous variables. The hard drive then needs to be reformatted, and when that happens and all the programs are removed, the computer is again restored to its original, untarnished state. Likewise, human beings can get corrupted by the complexities of society and life in the modern world, but they can easily return to their original, untainted state of love when they choose to abandon their attachments to the ego and things that are obstacles to the realization of their true self. These attachments include fear, doubt, worry, anxiety, hatred, resentment, envy, stress, depression —and anything that does not foster joy and peace.

Love is clearly something awesome embodying every person that is far greater than the genetic information stored in the DNA which resides in the nucleus of each human cell. Some refer to it as the vast intelligence that comprises our entire being, and some call it energy. Indeed, love is energy in its most fundamental sense— the raw material of all that is. It's the most profoundly essential and transformative energy, without which life itself would not be possible.

The loving nature of humans is a demonstrable fact. If you were to put two people, both strangers to each other, alone on a deserted island—they will eventually come to love each other. It's simply the nature of human beings to have the innate tendency and capacity to love.

But what about sociopaths, serial killers, wife beaters, child molesters, rapists, criminals, megalomaniacs or bigots who seem to be full of hatred, or show the desire to harm others or themselves—how could they possibly have a loving nature? They don't appear to have love because there are obstacles that prevent them from perceiving or expressing their essential nature, which is love. *Removing the blocks to their awareness of love's presence within them* is the key to creating dramatic transformations in their lives.

Likewise, if you're motivated by, or operating on things other than love, you simply have obstacles that keep you from seeing your loving nature. Love is like the bright sun that shines ceaselessly within you, and you just have to remove the clouds that hide its dazzling light. Love is the natural state that prevails when *fear*—and the other *obstacles* that prevent one from perceiving or expressing one's essential loving nature—are eradicated.

When you give *full expression* to the love that resides within, you unleash an *immeasurable power* and an *irresistible influence* that knows no bounds.

The *irony* of it all is that we as human beings have lost touch with that nature. We think love is just something we do, or something we give and receive, and not something **we are**. As a result, almost all our desires and aspirations center on *getting love*.

Consider why people would want to lose weight, for instance. Usually it's because they want to look good. Why do they want to look good? Because they want to gain the approval or admiration of others—or themselves. When you break their motives down further, you arrive at the one core reason why they do what they do. It's because deep down, what they truly want is love. They want other people to love them—and they want to love themselves.

The same holds true of our desire for success or wealth. Our desire for them all boils down to our need for love. And that's where the irony lies because as human beings, we already embody that which we seek —because we **are** love. Not just a doer of love, or a recipient of love but a *being* of love.

Love's Pathway

Being in a state of love is an absolute necessity if you want to be connected to the energy field which is responsible for the fulfillment of desires. The quality of *being loving* is not the same as *being love*, and neither does it have the same effect.

You might say that some of the most loving people that you've ever known hardly manifest their desires or live the good life. It's important to note that just because people seem loving doesn't mean they are in harmony with the energy field. They may display the *outward appearance* of lovingness, but it's possible that their loving behavior is motivated by insecurity, fear, a desperate need to be loved, pity, manipulation or control of others, to extract reciprocity or gain favor, or a host of other things that have nothing to do with love. There are also some people who are masters at the conspicuous display of generosity and kindness, which may be done for the admiration and applause of people —and not born out of genuine love. And then, of course, there are those who are fundamentally loving, but their prevalent thoughts center on low-energy emotions such as shame, anger, guilt, fear, frustration, resentment or judgment. In all of these cases, the individual is not *being* love but simply *going through the motions* of love, thereby never really connecting to the energy field.

The best way to connect to the energy field and remove the obstacles to the awareness of love's presence within one's self is by doing the following *powerful* exercise that I call **Love's Pathway**:

1) Close your eyes and breathe deeply 3 or 4 times, while saying the following to yourself: *I am the full expression of God's love. Just as God is love, so am I. I am love.*

2) Hold in mind the image of someone you love. This could be a family member, a spouse, boyfriend, girlfriend or significant other. Then imagine yourself putting your arms around that person in a loving embrace while simultaneously saying "I love you" in your mind. Hold on to this feeling of love, allowing it to spread throughout your entire being.

3) While holding on to this feeling of love, silently say to yourself, "I feel love." After a few moments mentally say, "I feel God." Then finally, in your

mind say, "Thank you," allowing the feeling of gratitude and appreciation to wash over you.

4) Remain in this state of *being* love for a few minutes, imagining the love in you radiating outward in an egg-shaped sphere of vibratory energy that flows out onto all people, encompassing the world and the universe.

You may repeat the process, holding in mind the image of another loved one in the next cycle, and still another loved one in the next cycle. You can do, as I do —and practice several cycles, going through every member of your family in succession. Or you can choose to do just one cycle—holding in mind thoughts of the person who naturally and easily causes strong feelings of love to be generated within you.

The profound effect of the above exercise cannot be emphasized enough. It may seem disarmingly simple, but it awakens in you feelings you didn't know you had. You'll learn the secrets of your heart, and the extent to which you can love another human being, and truly love yourself. It will also magnify the love that you already have for those you love and create a deeper bond between you and them.

Allow me to walk you through the various stages of the exercise, and what each step accomplishes.

➲ When you breathe deeply 3 or 4 times, this enables you to *center yourself,* silence your mind, and remove all extraneous thoughts and feelings in preparation for the exercise. As you contemplate on the truth that you, as a human being, are the full expression of God's love, you gain a newfound view of yourself that defies description. You'll feel a dismantling of your self-imposed imprisonment of pride and the ego-based emotions of resentment, fear, doubt, worry, greed or hatred.

➲ When you hold in mind the image of someone you love, this immediately puts your body in a state of strength. The science of applied kinesiology, pioneered by Dr. George Goodheart in the latter part of the 20th century, shows through muscle testing that certain stimuli increase the strength of certain indicator muscles while other stimuli would cause those same muscles to weaken. Emotional stimuli, such as picturing someone you love, provokes a demonstrably strong muscle response when compared to negative or neutral stimuli.

When you imagine putting your arms around a loved one while at the same time silently saying, "I love you", and then allowing the feeling of love to spread throughout your entire being, this act of loving another human being allows you to spontaneously detach from your identification with the ego momentarily because you're focusing on your loved one. Since, at that very moment, you're loving someone without condition or expectation of reciprocity, you step outside of yourself and transcend the ego for the time being.

Different people have different triggers that cause them to have deep feelings of love. Many of us respond to the sense of touch—therefore, envisioning a loving embrace or a gentle caress is just the key. For others, the deepest feeling of love is triggered when they say or hear the words, "I love you." In this step, feel free to add whatever it is that causes you to have deep feelings of love.

This is the emotional phase of the exercise. It allows you to start with the *feelings* of love that you're already familiar with, and use them as a *catalyst* for accessing the deeper dimensions of love that reside within you.

⊃ When you say to yourself, "I feel love" it brings crystal clear realization that something inside of you, your true loving nature, is finding full expression. When you say, "I feel God," a shift in awareness occurs as you realize you've found the bridge—the "wormhole", if you will—between emotional and spiritual dimensions, and you've opened the doorway to God through love.

When you say, "Thank you," it is an expression of profound gratitude and appreciation for the spiritual vision to see who you really are, and to revel in your boundless capacity to love. By *being* love, you connect to the energy field from which everything, including the manifestation of your desires, originates.

⊃ When you remain in the state of being love and imagine radiating love outward, you raise your frequency of vibration so that it ultimately becomes a vibrational match to the energy field, which means you've realigned yourself with the field.

"There is no mistaking love. You feel it in your heart. It is the common fiber of life, the flame that heats our soul, energizes our spirit and supplies passion to our lives. It is our connection to God and to each other."

—Elizabeth Kubler-Ross,
The Wheel of Life (Scribner)

Conscious connection to the energy field can happen in a *split* second. Many people are able to catch glimpses of this connection for brief moments—or maybe a few minutes, hours or days—when they are in an altered state of consciousness, or when they are experiencing a spiritual epiphany or a religious experience. It's characterized by that sublime, surreal feeling that everything is right in the world, that one has access to all the wisdom in the universe, and that anything one sets out to do will meet with success. While it's wonderful to experience that euphoric feeling of being connected, unless you can sustain that state longer than just a momentary period, it's nothing more than a spiritual "high" that will do little towards the fulfillment of your heart's desires.

When you awaken to the full realization that *you are love*, and practice the *Love's Pathway* exercise regularly, you *perpetuate* that state—and it becomes the "normal cruising altitude" of your life. That's when miracles begin to happen, and you experience the definition of self-realization referred to by Swami Paramananda, as follows: "Self-realization means that we have been consciously connected with our source of being. Once we have made this connection, then nothing can go wrong."

There are many ways of arriving at that conscious connection with the energy field. Often, it takes a lifetime of spiritual agony and suffering, combined with the performance of traditional spiritual practices. The recovery of millions of people from the incurable malady of alcoholism, for instance, follows a spiritually-based pathway called the 12-step program. Indeed, most people who have been cured of alcoholism using the 12 steps espoused by Alcoholics Anonymous (and embraced by other groups like Narcotics Anonymous, Gamblers Anonymous and Overeaters Anonymous) attribute their sobriety to a transformation of consciousness that they call a "spiritual experience." The spiritual experience involves, among other things, asking a power greater than themselves for strength and guidance, and daily prayer and meditation to *improve conscious contact with God.*

It should be noted that neither medicine, psychiatry, nor any branch of modern science, has ever been able to bring about the recovery from alcoholism that the spiritual truths of the 12-step program have been able to accomplish successfully. Likewise, neither positive thoughts and feelings, visualization, affirmations and any of the other techniques currently taught in conjunction with the Law of Attraction will ever wield the manifestation power of the *spiritual truths* contained herein. Consciously connecting with the energy field *through love* is the *accelerated* method—the sudden emergence into higher awareness, which dramatically shortens the time it takes to manifest desires. When you cast a pebble of love in the ocean of life, the ripples you create will return to you in waves, according to your heart's desires. If you cast no pebbles, there will be no waves to propel your heart's desires and enable them to arrive at your shores.

I'll never forget the first time I did the *Love's Pathway* exercise. It was just before I went to bed on a week night. As I went about picturing my loved ones, tears streamed down my face continuously as I beheld the true beauty of love. I had thought myself a loving person prior to the exercise, but that night, in just a few minutes, I experienced a spectacular breakthrough, more profound than anything I had previously known. There simply was nothing in my ordinary existence that compared to it. I emerged from the exercise with the infinite presence of an exquisite peace and a brand new set of eyes—eyes that saw in each person, beneath imperfect appearances, the shining magnificence of love and beauty. I became convinced I had become another person altogether—and that I had arrived at an enlightened sphere of consciousness, where I was at once the lover and the loved. I realized this place was the rarefied air of the quantum field, Source Energy, the field of all possibilities—of God—with which I had become one. I finally understood that this place inside of me is where truth prevails—and where God lives. I knew then that all things were, are and will always be possible for me.

I experienced a previously unattained level of spiritual awareness upon the very first practice, and have only become better with each succeeding session of *Love's Pathway*.

Love, in this context, doesn't simply mean other people's love for you (although the love of other people is often a catalyst in healing). It doesn't imply sitting around passively waiting for someone to love you. It actually refers to your own *capacity to love*—and this comes from removing the obstacles to the awareness of love's presence within one's self. When those obstacles are removed, one discovers a deep and abiding love and reverence for one's self, as well as for others. This spiritual love, then, goes beyond emotion and beyond the outward appearance of lovingness – but is rather a state of *being "in love"*—being within the divine matrix of love. It is not dependent on someone else's love for you. If people love you, that's wonderful—but if they don't, you find it in yourself to love them anyway. As your spiritual awareness grows, you begin to discover that "being loved" goes beyond having someone love you, and even beyond loving yourself—but it is an energy that you are a part of—the same energy that created the universe and everything that's in it. Ultimately, you realize that this energy field of inexhaustible love is within you—and within you also resides the source of your happiness.

When you become connected to this inexhaustible supply of love, you're able to heal yourself by becoming aware of the importance of love as a healing factor. It should be noted that every advanced spiritual seeker knows that at certain levels of spiritual awareness, physical diseases spontaneously become healed and pain instantly disappears. There is no scientific explanation for this but my spiritual understanding leads me to believe thus: Love and illness cannot coexist. Illness is simply the absence of love, and is vanquished by the presence of love.

You are also able to heal other people who are unable to heal themselves. Sometimes, all that is necessary to heal another person is just to love them at the spiritual level. You connect to the loving essence of the ill person, *allow* them to heal by their own recognition that they are loved, and enable them to realize that love is an important factor in their healing.

This healing phenomenon goes well beyond the grasp of science and medicine, and occurs by virtue of the spiritual power of the field. One should not attempt to do this in place of necessary medical attention, however, and before an adequate level of spiritual awareness has been achieved.

> "Where there is great love
> there are always miracles."
> —Willa Cather

The opposite of love is not hatred. It is fear. Love is the natural state when fear is eradicated. Conversely, fear is the most common obstacle that keeps us from being aware of love's presence within us. The *Love's Pathway* exercise helps tremendously in removing fear because fear is simply an ego-based emotion, and consistent practice of the *Love's Pathway* exercise allows one to transcend the ego.

When you transcend fear, love becomes as effortless as a spacecraft breaking through the earth's gravitational field and finding itself floating in the sublime weightlessness of outer space. The accompanying state of bliss is not unlike the feeling of one's self dissolving into a oneness with God and with all creation. Love goes far beyond the realm that the mind can comprehend, and enters into the domain of the spirit.

The ideal place for you to practice the *Love's Pathway* exercise is anywhere you can step away from the hustle and bustle of the world, and have some peace and quiet without interruptions. However, you may also practice short sessions anytime throughout the day, whenever you have a minute or two, even while standing in line at the supermarket or the post office, or in between repetitions at the gym. The more often you practice it, the better.

When you practice *Love's Pathway* on the people you love, have no desire but to love them for love's own sake. Let go of your need to manipulate or control their thinking, feelings or attitudes, and relinquish your desire to have them adjust themselves to make you happy. Just surround them with an unconditional love that requires no reciprocity. You'll begin to witness miracles happening when you let go of your attachment to the outcome produced by your love.

If the spirit moves you, you may even want to practice *Love's Pathway* on total strangers that you meet on the street, or anyone who you think is in need of love, such as a family member with whom you have a strained relationship, a rude waitress, your mean boss, a vindictive rival, or that condescending mom in your child's softball team. The rewards are endless when you make love a habit that you do all day long. You'll also find that miracles will become an everyday occurrence.

You'll know you've fully unmasked your true loving nature when you begin to see the world and everything in it as being beautiful. This means you've seen within yourself the beauty of who you are—the beauty of love. And you project onto the world what you see inside.

When you *are* love, your world is simply a reflection of what you've become.

 Chapter 6

How to Infuse Your Life with the Greatest Manifestation Principle

1) Cultivating the Most Important Relationship of All

Some people consider a loving relationship with their spouse, child, parent, sibling, boyfriend/girlfriend or friend their primary relationship. But there is an even more important relationship that needs to be developed before you can expect your relationships with other people to be truly fruitful and free of conflict. That is the relationship you have with yourself.

Your relationship with yourself directs the course and determines the success or failure of your relationships with other people. In cultivating a relationship with yourself, because your true self is *love*, you are developing a deep connection with the source of love, which is God (whom I've referred to as the *energy field* throughout this book). Therefore, endeavor to consciously connect with your source of being so that your vibrational energy matches up to that of God from whom all good things come.

You cannot discover in another person what you can't first discover in yourself. Whatever you perceive in yourself is what you project upon other people, and by extension, the world. If you see imperfection in others, you haven't been made perfect in love. You know you've found beauty and love in yourself only when you see beauty and love in all people, including those who might appear unattractive to others and those who are unlovable.

You can find beauty and love in yourself by moving yourself into the field of awareness that you are love. The *Love's Pathway* exercise can help you accomplish this. Knowing your true identity is one of the most life-altering realizations you will ever have in your life. The pure, resplendent joy of **being** love, and the profound peace that accompanies it, is your true wealth.

Extend your love upon your circle of family, friends and acquaintances, and let it expand to everyone you meet or interact with in your community and the world. Show kindness towards all of life in all of its expressions, including yourself. Be willing to forgive

116

yourself and other people, and endeavor to perceive each person as having the same loving nature as you. Practice loving those who have hurt or offended you or caused you to experience suffering. When you are able to love all people and all things, you *become* love, and you attract to yourself all good things that are a vibrational match to love.

2) Surrendering to the Divine

Accessing your true self may prove to be difficult when the challenges of life and ego-based emotions get in the way. Ease comes when you surrender every aspect of yourself to the divine. When you do this, you'll experience a significant shift in your personal world and the world at large.

Surrender not only your pain, suffering, resentment, anger, self-pity, grief, victimization, the feeling of being wronged, being offended, being cheated on, being taken advantage of—but also your personal agenda and your desires—as they arise. Surrender *the way you see things* and trust that when you remain consciously connected with the energy field (God), you will perceive a more magnificent view of the world than

117

you've ever seen, and gain access to the infinite power of the energy field.

Let go of all resistance to the flow of life. Your job is to be in harmony at all times with the energy field through love. When you impose your standards, expectations and preconceived notions on what and how the universe will deliver its bounty to you, you virtually set up barriers that keep you from getting all the good things the energy field has in store for you.

Above all, surrender your fears whenever they arise. Fear is a denial of the existence of the divine power that resides within you—the divine power of which you are a part. And fear is the low energy that obscures the presence of love. Be willing to step away from the ego-based emotion of fear, as well as everything that stands in the way of your awareness of the divinity that lives in you. Escaping to the realm of love will not only restore your energy, but also bring you immense peace.

It is human nature to take a position on anything—or labeling anything as either good or bad, healthy or unhealthy, or something being this as opposed to that. The moment you *label* a person, event, circumstance or thing as being a certain way, you set up a reaction to it.

For example, if you label an event as disappointing, you instantly assume the position of resisting the disappointment. It's the way you've labeled it—and the accompanying resistance—that causes something to be experienced as disappointing. The moment you surrender your position, let go of your resistance and consciously connect to the field, that person, event, circumstance or thing ceases to be disappointing. The source of the disappointment stems from the *way you see things* and *label things*. With constant surrender, however, virtually all things that you regard as undesirable—including illness, lack, hostility, heartbreak and other challenging issues vanish—and your life becomes transformed.

3) Everything is As It Should Be

In the quest to manifest our desires, we often demand that the world—and all the people and things in it—be different from what they presently are. We want things to change in order to suit our purposes and fit our idea of order and perfection—so we try to fix the world and control others in order to accomplish it. This constitutes *resistance* to the flow of the universe.

You make a difference in your world <u>not</u> by trying to fix things according to your wishes and specifications. At any given moment, everything is as it should be, based on the energy you've sown or not sown. Therefore, there's no sense in resisting the way things are. Instead, the way to make the biggest impact on your world is by focusing your efforts on raising your own level of consciousness, being in touch with your true self and being connected to the Source. Doing so frees up your energy from wasteful preoccupations and enables you to use it for creative purposes. It also allows the energy of the universe to flow—unimpeded by your resistance.

With the exception of children, who rightfully need to be trained until they reach the age of self-sufficiency, let go of your desire to change people to suit your purposes. Accept the fact that you cannot *make* people do something they're not *naturally predisposed* to doing, nor can you *cause* them to become anyone other than who they are. To do so would entail the use of threat, demands, punishment, manipulation, persuasion or other devices that employ some manner of control or force. There are psychological principles and relationship strategies that might seem to produce behavioral modifications in people, but those changes are not likely to last if they're not tied to the true nature of people.

We, as human beings, tend to view other people merely as a means to our desired ends—as though they existed solely to serve our purposes. Love is often so glaringly absent in our interactions with people, and we focus instead on how well (or how poorly) our own needs are being met—seldom thinking about the human beings with whom we are interacting, and seldom caring about them more than we care about ourselves.

Endeavor to hold all people you encounter in the highest regard—<u>not</u> because of what you hope they can do for you, nor the needs you hope they can meet, or for any reason other than just because you behold their magnificence as spiritual beings whom you treasure and love far beyond what you perceive as their usefulness to you. Let every thought of them, every word you speak to them, and everything you do for them and with them become imbued with love.

Again, the only way you can make an important difference in people's lives is by moving yourself into the field of awareness that you are love and by removing all the obstacles which keep you from identifying yourself as *being* love. Love must begin as a flame that you reignite within yourself before you can influence others to reignite it within themselves.

4) The World's Rules of Economy Do Not Apply

The world's rules of economy are based on the exchange of goods and services. Each party in a transaction brings goods, services or funds to the table, and each receives something in return that represents a fair and equitable exchange. Because this model works very well in most instances, we often try to apply the fairness principle on our relationships. More often than not, this becomes the source of a relationship problem. Two people in a relationship rarely contribute an equal amount of time, resources or devotion to a relationship, and when this inequity happens, someone ends up feeling shortchanged, resentment builds, and discord results. "But that's not fair!" and "What about my needs?" become common anthems. The ego rears its head, and the individuals involved in a relationship begin to entertain feelings of being taken for granted, being used, being wronged—and other expressions of being offended.

Love's economy doesn't operate in this kind of give-and-take relay. If it did, love wouldn't endure. If the love of a mother for her infant child depended on what the infant contributed to the mother-child relationship, there would be no such thing as motherly love. By the same token, if the love of a woman for a man depended on whether a man fulfilled her needs or not, there will oftentimes be a deficit—either real or imagined—from the woman's viewpoint. The fulfillment of needs has never been, nor will it ever be, the ideal standard for perpetuating love in a relationship.

In our narcissistic culture, it is often difficult to view another person's "reality" as being just as important as our own. We tend to focus on what we are getting, how *we* are being treated, and what's in it for *us*—and we usually perceive other people's lives in terms of how they affect our own lives. Develop the practice of focusing on other people instead. What can you do to add to their well-being, or make their lives more joyful? This practice enables you to step outside of yourself and want just as much for other people as you want for yourself—or more. This is the beginning of true power.

The bottom line is that one cannot use the world's rules of economy—nor can you use psychology or any standards of the physical world to govern something that does not belong in the physical or mental realm. Love belongs in the realm of the soul.

Love is complete in and of itself, lacking nothing —and requiring nothing from that which it loves. Therein lies another important distinction between the world view and the spiritual view. The world sees a relationship as being successful when the needs of both parties in the relationship are mutually fulfilled. "You give me what I need, and I give you what you need." Unconditional love, on the other hand, needs nothing but to seek the full expression of itself.

5) The Key to Happiness

In a previous chapter, I mentioned that the best way to have your desires fulfilled is to let go of those desires. According to kinesiological muscle testing, being in a state of desire weakens a person. Desire ranks 6th to the lowest among the levels of enlightenment in the Map of Consciousness developed by David Hawkins,

M.D., Ph.D.—even lower than pride and anger. It calibrates below the level of neutrality, together with other weakening, low-frequency emotions such as shame, guilt, apathy, grief and fear.

Inherent in every desire is the unconscious belief that the fulfillment of the desire will bring you happiness. This belief makes you dependent on external conditions —and therefore, you're always in a weak and vulnerable position, always fearful that your happiness is at the whim of something or someone else. If, instead, you strive for self-fulfillment through conscious connection with the energy field, which is the source of all things, then no one can take your happiness away from you.

Let go of the state of "wanting" and be in the state of "having" or "accepting" instead. The only reason you desire something is because you think you can find happiness outside of yourself. If you get your dream car, then you'll feel proud driving it around, then you'll be happy. If you get a dream job, you'll feel successful, then you'll be happy. If you win the lottery, you'll be rich, then you'll be happy.

This illusion of happiness seems true only because we're conditioned to define happiness through external conditions like luck, good fortune, or the favor or approval we receive from people. It even infiltrates the language we use in our everyday lives. We say things like, "I'm so happy that my boss gave me a raise," or "My husband/wife makes me so happy" or "Owning my dream house makes me happy" or "Being successful in my chosen career makes me happy." These statements presuppose that something outside of ourselves makes us happy when in actuality, it is how we *represent* the event, person, or circumstance to our own mind that brought about the state of happiness.

> "We represent the world to ourselves and respond to our representations."
> —The Crack in the Cosmic Egg, Joseph Chilton Pearce

Happiness is <u>not</u> an emotion that is caused by people, events or circumstances. It is a state that we choose to create in ourselves, *sometimes* as a result of people, events and circumstances. We've been conditioned to rely on external things to make us happy, when in fact, we don't have to wait for them to happen to us in order to be happy. Since we already know that happiness is something we choose to create, based on how we represent circumstances to our own mind, it stands to reason that you can choose to create happiness anytime, without waiting for luck or good fortune to come around, or before your desires are manifested.

Ultimately, it is you and you alone who can make you happy. This is true of all negative emotional states as well—you alone can make yourself become fearful, anxious, doubtful, stressed out or full of worry. You choose to create them within yourself, or you choose to eliminate them from your awareness.

Eliminating negative emotional states from your awareness becomes easy when you realize that your thoughts and emotions are <u>not</u> who you *are*. Thoughts, and the emotions that they wield, are simply mental constructs that have no meaning except the meaning you give them. You are the *witness* or the *observer* of your thoughts and emotions. It is your ego (your false self) that is doing the "thinking" based on its illusory idea of who you are. Left to its own devices, the ego will speculate, ruminate, overanalyze and rehash what could have, would have or should have occurred—not unlike a dog chasing its own tail. Like it or not, you are *mesmerized* by this endless succession of "mental entertainment" because you get some kind of perverted pleasure from satisfying your egocentricity. Instead of preoccupying yourself with the event, person or situation that your ego has perceived as being the cause of your negative emotional state, *separate yourself from your ego* and realize that you are the *spectator* of the thinking. *Watch* your thoughts and emotions as a parent would watch the behavior of a boisterous child.

Remember that just as you are not your thoughts and emotions, you also are not your possessions, your livelihood, your accomplishments or your reputation. Love is your true self. Therefore, let love—and not worldly preoccupations—define you.

Above all, don't put your happiness on hold until all the circumstances in your life become perfect—or until your desires manifest. Do not take the position of waiting for your fortune to change before you become happy. Reverse-engineer your life by being happy now. Happiness begets more happiness—and attracts an avalanche of the positive conditions you want in your life.

If you are someone who wants to lose weight,

eliminate procrastination, become more productive, get rid of mental obsessions or addictions, resolve marital and personal relationship problems—and rise above any and all human dilemmas—the solution is as simple as consciously connecting to the field of all possibilities using the spiritual truths revealed in this book. Before long, you'll find yourself behaving in ways that would naturally cause those things to happen.

Surrender to prevalent circumstances in your life instead of trying to change them. When you're thankful for all things and infuse everything with love, you gain something that is exceedingly and abundantly more than you could ever ask, think or imagine.

> "Neither a lofty degree of intelligence nor imagination nor both together go to the making of genius. Love, love, love, that is the soul of genius."
> —Wolfgang Amadeus Mozart

If we were told we only have 10 minutes left before the end of the world, what would we do with that time? We would tell our loved ones that we love them. And yet in our busy workaday world, sometimes we allow days, weeks and months to go by without expressing our love to those whom we love. Do it today. Let love begin as a flame that you light within you. Love yourself first, and then spread that love beyond yourself and out into the world. Because at the end of our lives, we'll want to remember not how well we lived but how well we loved.

As I come to the end of this book, it is my wish that I've impressed upon you that when you apply the greatest manifestation principle of love to the Law of Attraction, your desires have the greatest likelihood of manifesting. When your desires are *motivated* and *nourished* by love—and you *stay connected* to the energy field through love—your desires MUST manifest because love is the most powerful magnetic force in the universe that attracts miraculously wonderful things to you that are often greater than your desires.

But the greatest miracle, by far, is that as you become fully aware of love's presence within you, you'll discover the greatest joy of all—that love is its own reward. When you realize that your capacity to love comes from the divine presence within you, and that love is God's way of affording you a glimpse of his own unfathomable love, you'll know without a doubt that God's creative power is available to you every time you choose to love.

If you enjoyed this book, you may wish to …

✓ Share your comments at
www.GreatestManifestationPrinciple.com/readerscorner.htm

or

✓ Order copies to give away as gifts by going to
www.GreatestManifestationPrinciple.com/order.htm

For discount pricing on order quantities of 10 or
more, please send an e-mail to
quantitydiscounts@GreatestManifestationPrinciple.com

or contact

Think-Outside-the-Book Publishing, Inc.
311 N. Robertson Boulevard, Suite 323
Beverly Hills, California 90211

Other books by Carnelian Sage:
"The Love Effect"
http://www.TheLoveEffect.com